Spanish Proficiency Practice

by

Ronnie Maibaum

Rockaway Beach Junior High School, Rockaway Park, New York (ret.)
Queens College, City University of New York, Flushing, New York

Magali Alvarez

Elizabeth Blackwell Middle School, Ozone Park, New York

Copyright © 2001 by CURRICULUM PRESS, INC.
Albany, New York
ISBN 0-941519-20-1

© 2001 by CURRICULUM PRESS, INC., Albany, New York. All rights reserved. No part of this book may be reproduced, stored in a retrieval system or transcribed, in any form or by any means, electronic, mechanical, photocopy, recording, or otherwise, without the express written consent of the publisher.
Printed in the United States of America.

TABLE OF CONTENTS

Introduction to Part 1...1
    Part 1A: Informal Speaking 2
    Part 1B: Formal Speaking 4
    Scoring Guidelines for Speaking 10
    Speaking Checklist 14
    The Quality Point 16
    Formal Speaking Models 17
    Let's Practice! 21

Introduction to Part 2 25
    Part 2A: Listening Comprehension, Questions in English 26
    Part 2A: Let's Practice! 29
    Part 2B: Listening Comprehension, Questions in Spanish 39
    Part 2B: Let's Practice! 41
    Part 2C: Listening Comprehension with Pictures 49
    Part 2C: Let's Practice! 51

Introduction to Part 3 60
    Part 3A: Reading Authentic Materials, Questions in English 61
    Part 3A: Let's Practice! 64
    Part 3B: Reading Authentic Materials, Questions in Spanish............. 70
    Part 3B: Let's Practice! 71
    Part 3C: Reading a Topical Passage 77
    Part 3C: Let's Practice! 79

Introduction to Part 4 87
    Part 4: Writing 88
    Scoring Guidelines for Writing 91
    Writing Checklist 94
    Writing Models 96
    Let's Practice! 99

Preface

As a study and practice guide to prepare for the New York State Second Language Proficiency examinations, this book will be of use to both students and teachers. Practice material is offered for all the skills (speaking, listening, reading and writing) to be tested, so that use of this book during the school year prior to the examination can reduce students' anxiety and help them to perform at a higher level. To ensure that students do as well as possible, frequent class use of activities similar to those presented is most beneficial.

Through this book students will become aware of the new requirements for proficiency and the standards of performance expected of them. Included here are activities they can do in class with the teacher or other students, and also independent practice they can do outside of school. They will be encouraged to use what they already know and what they are learning in the most productive ways.

To the student

You must remember that the Second Language Proficiency Examination is a test of knowledge and abilities acquired during your entire study of Checkpoint A—you can't cram for it the night before the test.

It is not an achievement test—you will not be asked to show what you know. You will be showing *what you can do* with what you know.

For this reason, this book is designed to help you understand the questions on the examination, the most acceptable kinds of answers, and how you will be scored.

Practicing with the sample questions throughout the year and measuring your work against the actual standards your teachers will use in scoring will allow you to discover which areas you do well in, and which skills you need to improve.

You should strive during the year to acquire a large *passive* vocabulary (understanding words when you see or hear them) as well as an *active* vocabulary (being able to use the words in original speech and writing).

Try to use all you have learned over time. The vocabulary you see in the exam may have been taught in a unit months ago.

You will be given simple specific suggestions as to how to approach each section of the examination to make the most of what you know. If you do the practice conscientiously on a continuing basis, you should be successful.

  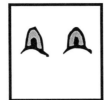 

Part 1
Speaking

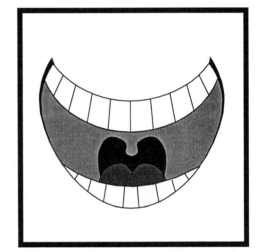

There are two sections of speaking ability tests:

Part 1A, Informal Test of Speaking Ability, and

Part 1B, Formal Test of Speaking Ability.

Both are scored with a set of guidelines that you will want to know about.

Part 1A
Informal Test of Speaking

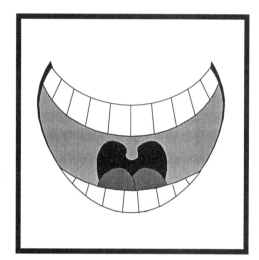

The question

A test of your informal speaking abilities is part of the examination, but it won't take place at the end of the year at a specific test time. Instead, your teacher will be paying close attention to your oral performance in class during the entire school year before the examination. You should be aware that your informal speaking will be scored by how *often* you speak in addition to how *well*.

The background

Worth 10 points, the informal speaking part of the examination will be scored with a new set of guidelines which take a lot of different things into account. Your speech will be evaluated based on the six *criteria* (standards for performance in the different areas) covered by the guidelines:

1. Sometimes you will be expected to start the conversation and respond to both questions and statements in an appropriate way.

2. You should be able to carry on conversations easily without relying on the person you are speaking with to prompt you.

3. You must be able to use a variety of vocabulary and everyday Spanish expressions, and use structures including verbs, noun and adjective agreement, and correct word order, with few errors.

4. You should also be able to demonstrate understanding of Spanish-speaking cultures in specific situations.

Almost *always* meeting these standards will result in the most credit for this part of the exam. The points you score will go down as you only *frequently*, *sometimes* or *rarely* meet these standards of performance.

Your goal during the year should be to improve as time passes. Be critical of yourself and be sure to ask your teacher for suggestions on how to strengthen your speaking skills. Only with daily practice can you expect to strengthen your abilities. Simply listening to others speak will not be enough.

The strategy

1. Take advantage of every opportunity to speak Spanish. Practice with your friends to prepare for class.

2. If you are shy about participating orally, speak Spanish aloud outside of school. Speaking into a tape recorder is especially good practice. This will help you get used to the sound of your voice speaking Spanish, and will let you listen to what you're doing right or wrong.

3. Participate daily in oral class work.

4. If conversation practice with other students is a part of daily class work, use it as an opportunity to learn and use correct vocabulary and structures.

5. Make an effort to be easy to understand even if you have some errors in pronunciation, vocabulary or structure.

6. Do not be afraid to correct yourself as you are speaking, if you realize you've made an error.

Part 1B
Formal Test of Speaking

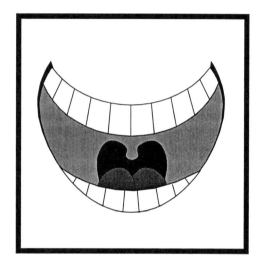

The question

This speaking task consists of four conversation tasks to be performed by students with their teacher. Each task consists of a brief statement in English which indicates the setting of the communication, the role of the teacher and the person who is to initiate the conversation. Each task must be completed in four interactions between the student and the teacher. [20 points]

The background

If you follow all the suggestions from the Informal Speaking section, you will also be well prepared for this part of the exam. Remember to participate orally on a regular basis in class and outside of class, with other students if possible, so that you don't find yourself tongue-tied and nervous.

You will be speaking one-to-one with your teacher four times, on topics you don't know until just before the conversations begin, so make sure you are alert and concentrating. In each conversation you will be required to provide four comprehensible utterances. Read the following section on scoring very carefully in order to understand how you can earn the most credit.

It is important that you start your part of the conversation successfully. Whether initiating or responding, **two** failures to support your part of the conversation will result in no credit for the whole conversation.

Once started, you are allowed two attempts for each of the remaining three utterances in order to earn credit.

The Quality Point, which is discussed later, enables you to earn five points for your conversation instead of four. The Quality Point ***cannot*** be earned if more than two of your utterances are second attempts.

Being easy to understand and appropriate for the testing topic are the main *criteria* (the specific items) in scoring. The Quality Point earns extra credit for overall spontaneity (being flexible and quick to respond), fluency, and accuracy as well as the strict standards applied to Part 1A.

In many schools, students will be tested with the rest of the class present. It may make you nervous to be tested while there are noises and distractions, so you can see how important it is to practice speaking until you feel confident.

Because this type of testing takes a lot of time, your teacher may not use it regularly as part of your normal unit tests. So whatever conversational practice you can get, in class or outside of school, becomes very important. All your classmates need to practice too, so make an effort to speak Spanish with them as often as possible. You don't have to make up situations. Base your practice on what you're covering in class. Divide your practice into these four categories: Socializing, Providing and Obtaining Information, Expressing Feelings and Opinions, and Persuasion. These are the categories the testing tasks are divided into.

The strategy

Remember, your teacher has your best interests in mind on this part of the examination. S/he will make every effort to help guide the conversation in directions that will help you.

Do not hesitate to *start a new direction* in the discussion if it makes sense. Do that, if possible, whenever you feel that a transition can be made to a more comfortable vocabulary area. For example:

1. The teacher states that it is almost time for lunch.

2. You feel uncomfortable with food expressions, so you agree, but then state that you want to watch the football team practice at lunch time.

In effect, you have shifted the direction of the conversation so you can use your more complete vocabulary about sports. You can talk about the football team's record, and compare them to the basketball team, or talk about which sport you prefer, and why. Your response was appropriate and complete, worthy of full credit. It has also made it necessary for the teacher to respond to your direction.

Here are additional strategies you can use to study for this part of the exam:

1. Practice different responses to the same opening line. Even something simple like "How are you?" can have more than one answer (I'm very well, thank you./I don't feel well./I'm sick.). More complex questions, such as "Where do you want to go after school?" are open to many choices (I want to go to the library./Let's play basketball./I have to go home.) which will lead the conversation in different directions.

2. Remember that you get two chances to gain full credit for an appropriate utterance. Your teacher will cue you when your response has been inappropriate. Take a deep breath, slow down, and try again. If you have to try more than twice to **start** the conversation, you cannot get credit for that speaking task.

3. Learn words and phrases that can be used appropriately in more than one situation. "I like that very much," can fit in many situations.

4. Learn to reply to statements as well as questions. You may also use statements when you are called on to start the conversation. For instance, if a conversation is about preferences in food, music, or classes, the teacher may begin with a statement "I like/don't like . . ." rather than a question, and you must respond by agreeing or disagreeing. (Remember that you must use a statement to agree or disagree, because a Yes/No answer will get 0 credit.)

If you are called on to begin a task, and you start with a statement, "I want to go to the park," instead of an open-ended question, "Where do you want to go?" you take control of the direction of the conversation and can lead it into your strong areas of knowledge.

5. Categorize statements, questions, and expressions by the functions the test tasks fall into: Socializing, Providing and Obtaining Information, Expressing Feelings and Opinions, and Persuasion. You might keep lists of these during the year.

What to do at testing time

1. Your teacher may choose tasks at random. If so, first you will want to figure out which group your task is in: Socializing ("What's your name?"), Providing and Obtaining Information ("Where is the Metro Station?"), Expressing Feelings and Opinions ("I don't like . . ."), or Persuasion ("Let's go to . . ."). This will help you choose vocabulary and structures.

2. Make the best use of your "thinking time." Think about the setting and the role your teacher is playing.

3. Even your simplest answers must fit the situation. Try to anticipate what will come up in the conversation. For example, in a clothing store there would be item, size, color, and price.

4. Recognize the *interrogatives* (question words) and the kinds of answers they will call for, since you won't be asked any questions that have Yes or No answers.

5. Stretch your knowledge by restricting each utterance to one fact. For example, "I want a one-way first-class ticket to Madrid" is a sentence that states three pieces of information. A better strategy is to give just the destination, and make the teacher get the other information. Those three facts plus a question to find out the cost of the ticket would make the four utterances needed for a successful conversation. Let's take a closer look:

Student: I want a ticket to Madrid. **(1)**
Teacher: Round-trip or one-way?
Student: One-way, please. **(2)**
Teacher: Which class?
Student: First class. **(3)**
Teacher: Here's your ticket.
Student: How much is it? **(4)**
Teacher: Four hundred pesetas.
Student: Thank you.

Common Expressions

This section contains common expressions in Spanish, grouped in the four categories for testing: Socializing, Providing and Obtaining Information, Expressing Feelings and Opinions, and Persuasion. It will help you greatly on the Formal Speaking exam if you become very familiar with these expressions, especially if *you associate the expression with the category*. Practicing with these expressions will help you find fresh and appropriate directions for your conversations.

Socializing

¿Cómo te llamas?   Me llamo . . .
¿Cómo estás?   Estoy bien. (cansado/a) (enfermo/a) (regular)
¿Cómo te sientes?   Me siento bien. (mal)
¿Qué te pasa?   Tengo dolor de cabeza. / Me duele la garganta.
¡Que te mejores pronto!   *Hope you feel better!*
Quiero presentarte(le) a . . .   *I want to introduce you to . . .*
    Encantado(a).   *Delighted.* / Mucho gusto.   *Pleased to meet you.*
Hace mucho tiempo que no te veo.   *I haven't seen you for a long time.*
¡Cuánto me alegro de verte!   *How happy I am to see you!*
¡Cuánto me alegro!   *How happy I am!*
¡Cuánto lo siento! / ¡Lo siento mucho!   *How sorry I am!*
Me gustaría.   *I would like to.*
No puedo.   *I can't.*
Está bien.   *Okay.*
Se me hace tarde.   *It's getting late.*
¡Que le vaya bien!   *Hope all goes well for you!*
¡Que lo pases bien!   *Hope you have a good time!*
Gracias por . . .   *Thanks for . . .*

Providing and Obtaining Information

All interrogatives with appropriate answers:

¿Dónde . . . ?   *Where . . . ? (places)*
¿Quién . . . ?   *Who . . . ? (people)*
    ¿Con quién . . . ?   *With whom . . . ?*
¿Cuánto . . . ?   *How much . . . ? (number)*
    ¿Por cuánto tiempo . . . ?   *How long . . . ?*
    ¿Cuántos/as . . . ?   *How many . . . ?*

¿Cuándo . . . ?   *When . . . ? (time)*
¿Cómo . . . ?   *How . . . ? (adjectives, adverbs)*
¿Qué . . . ?   *What . . . ?*
    ¿Qué haces . . . ?   *What do you do . . . ? (activities)*
    ¿A qué hora . . . ?   *At what time . . . ?*

¿Cuál...? *Which...?*   ¿Por qué...? *Why...? (reason)*
  ¿Cuál es...? *What is...? / Which one is...?*
¿Qué sabes de...? *What do you know about...?*
¿Me puede ayudar? *Can you help me?*
Necesito... *I need...*

Expressing Feelings and Opinions

Me gusta... *I like...*   No me gusta... *I don't like...*
¿Qué te(le) gusta más? *What do you like the most?*
Me encanta... *I love to...*
Prefiero... *I prefer...*   ¿Qué prefieres? *What do you prefer?*
Me gustaría... *I would like to...*
No me gustaría porque... *I wouldn't like to because...*
¿Cuál es tu... favorito(a)? *What is your favorite...?*
Quiero... *I want...*
Tengo ganas de... *I feel like...*
Estoy cansado(a) de... *I'm tired of...*
Vale la pena. *It's worthwhile.*
Yo también. *Me too.*   Ni yo tampoco. *Me neither.*
¿Es verdad? *Is it true?*   Es verdad. *It's true.*   No es verdad. *It's not true.*
Tienes razón. *You are right.*   No tienes razón. *You are wrong.*
¿Qué piensas de...? *What do you think of...?*
Creo que... *I believe that...*   No creo que... *I don't believe that...*
¿Qué te parece? *What do you think?*   Me parece bien. *I think it's fine.*
¡Claro que sí! / ¡Por supuesto! / ¡Cómo no! *Of course!*
Está bien. *Okay.*   Buena idea. *Good idea.*   De acuerdo. *I agree.*
¡Qué lástima! *What a pity!*
¡Cuánto me alegro! *How happy I am!*
¡Cuánto lo siento! *How sorry I am!*

Persuasion

Vamos a... *Let's...*
¿Por qué no vamos a...? *Why don't we go to...?*
¿Qué te parece si...? *What do you think if...?*
¿Por qué no puedes...? *Why can't you...?*
Tú debes... *You ought to...*
Vale la pena... *It's worthwhile...*
Lo mejor es... *The best thing is to...*
Favor de... *Please...*
Tengo una buena idea. *I have a good idea.*

PART 1A — Scoring Your Speaking Ability

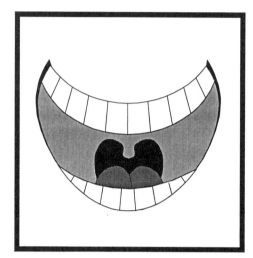

How will your speaking be scored? You can get a score of from 0 (lowest) to 4 points (highest) in six different areas. A score of 0 in any area means the speech did not include enough material for a score of 1 point. Here are the areas in which you'll be scored, and what performance you must deliver to get each score:

Initiation (Starting the conversation)

4 points:
> You have no problem starting conversations on your own and keeping them going without help.

3 points:
> You are able to begin speaking and ask questions on your own with very few problems.

2 points:
> You sometimes have problems starting to speak and keeping conversations going.

1 point:
> You have trouble beginning to speak and find it hard to continue the conversation.

Response

4 points:
> You have no problems answering when someone speaks to you.

3 points:
> You have no problems most of the time when someone speaks to you.

2 points:
> You sometimes have problems answering correctly when someone speaks to you.

1 point:
> You always have problems answering correctly when someone speaks to you.

Conversational Strategies

4 points:
> You are able to use different ways to help yourself keep a conversation going when you have problems with words or grammar. For example:
> - You use words you know to describe words you forget or don't know.
> - You ask for things to be repeated or explained to you.
> - You use your voice to show the difference between a question and a statement.
> - You correct your own mistakes when you realize you are making them.
> - You listen to what your partner says to help you with what you want to say.

3 points:
> You are able to help yourself, but do better when your partner gives you an idea.

2 points:
> You can sometimes help yourself, but you depend too much on your partner to give you ideas.

1 point:
> You have trouble keeping the conversation going yourself, even with a lot of help from your partner.

Vocabulary

4 points:
> You use a lot of different words and phrases in your conversation, and pronounce everything very well.

3 points:
> You try to use a lot of different words and phrases in your conversation and to pronounce everything correctly.

2 points:
> You use very simple words and phrases in your conversation and even though you make some mistakes in pronunciation, it isn't hard to understand you.

1 point:
> You use very few words in your conversation and the way you pronounce them makes it hard to understand what you want to say.

Structure

4 points:
> You make almost no mistakes when you conjugate verbs, when you use nouns and adjectives together, and when you put words in order in sentences. Any mistakes you make don't make it hard to understand what you want to say.

3 points:
> You make some mistakes, but it still isn't hard to understand what you want to say.

2 points:
> You make some mistakes, and they are the kind that make it hard to follow what you are saying.

1 point:
> You use so few words and phrases that you show you don't know much language and it makes it very hard to understand what you mean.

Cultural Appropriateness

4 points:
>You show that you understand the customs of native speakers when you say and do things correctly when they are right for a specific situation.

3 points:
>You show that you know what to say and do in situations most of the time.

2 points:
>You sometimes have problems knowing when to say and do the correct thing in a situation.

1 point:
>You almost never show that you understand what would be correct in different situations.

Speaking Checklist

Now that you have read and understood the details of how you will be scored, here is the "short form" checklist that your teacher will use to score your speaking ability. Learn this well! After you become familiar with it, you might even want to follow this list as you or a study partner practice speaking activities, and give the activity a score.

4   3   2   1   0

Initiation

- Do you begin the conversation on your own?
- Do you say something to get the conversation started?
- Do you say everything without help?

Response

- Do your answers to your partner's questions make sense?

	4	3	2	1	0

Conversational Strategies

- Do you need help to keep the conversation going?
- Do you use any of these ways to help yourself when you are speaking?
    - Do you use words you know to describe words you forgot or don't know?
    - Do you ask for anything to be repeated or explained to you?
    - Do you use your voice to show the difference between a question and a statement?
    - Do you correct any of your own mistakes when you realize you've made them?
    - Do you listen to and use what your partner says to help you with what you want to say?

Vocabulary

- Do you use a lot of different kinds of words?
- Do you use common expressions connected to the topic?
- Does your pronunciation make it hard to understand what you say?

Structure

(Do your mistakes make it hard to understand what you're saying?)
- Do you use the right form of the verbs for different subjects?
- Do you match nouns with the right form of adjectives?
- Do you put the words in the right order in sentences?

Cultural Appropriateness

- Do you show you understand customs of native speakers by what you say and do during the conversation?

Part 1B
Quality Point

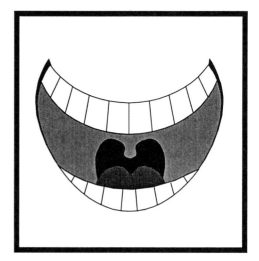

The "Quality Point" is an extra point your teacher can give you for each formal conversation, depending on how well you do your part in completing the task.

If, at three different times in the conversation, your teacher has to try more than twice to get you to say something to respond to a question or statement, you can't receive the extra point.

Your part of the conversation must show all the following things to earn the extra point.

Fluency

You keep the conversation going (in *Spanish!*) without your partner's help. Your pronunciation is good, your tone of voice changes for questions and statements, and your speech fits the situation.

Complexity

You use a lot of different words to make up questions and statements that are original, without waiting for your partner. You conjugate verbs correctly and don't make very many grammatical errors.

Accuracy

Someone who is a native speaker of Spanish could understand what you say. If you hear yourself make a mistake you correct it. The words you use are right for the situation, and the grammatical errors you make aren't the kind that make it hard to understand you.

Part 1
Models for Speaking Tasks

In this section, we will take a look at two sample speaking topics and two different student answers. We will show you how each answer would be scored, and why one earned the Quality Point, and the other did not.

Example

The student has chosen this socializing task at random:

(Teacher initiates) Teacher says: I am your friend. I want to invite you to a party. I will start the conversation.

Presentation of Task

Teacher Says in English	**Student Says in English**
I am your friend. I want to invite you to a party. I will start the conversation. Do you understand the situation?	Yes, I do.

All right. Remember, I'll be inviting you to a party. I'll give you a few seconds to think about what you might want to say in Spanish in this situation. (Short pause) Are you ready?   Yes, I am.

From now on, we'll use no more English.

Task Begins (All in Spanish)

Teacher Says	Student Says	Rating
Quiero invitarte a mi fiesta de cumpleaños.		
	Sí.	**"Yes-No" response**: Disregard. Teacher makes first eliciting attempt again.
Es la semana que viene.		
	¿Qué día de la semana?	**1 credit:** Comprehensible and appropriate.
Es el domingo por la tarde.		
	¿Qué hora es?	**1 credit:** Comprehensible and appropriate (even with error).
Empieza a las tres en mi casa.		
	¿Tu casa?	**Restatement**: Disregard. Teacher makes eliciting attempt again.
Sí, tú sabes mi dirección.		
	No donde dirección.	**0 credit for this utterance.** Second attempt is inappropriate. Teacher makes first eliciting attempt for Utterance #4.
Yo te doy la dirección. Vamos a escuchar música y bailar. Vamos a divertirnos.		
	Bueno. Yo gusto bailar.	**1 credit.** Comprehensible and appropriate. Grammatical error doesn't hinder comprehension.

Quality Point

No Quality Point earned because:

1. Student needed several second eliciting attempts.

2. Student made several structure and vocabulary errors.

3. Student had difficulty keeping the conversation moving.

4. Student used very few words in the conversation.

Credit for Task: 3 points

Example II

The student has chosen this persuasion task at random:

(Student initiates) Teacher says: I am your friend. We are discussing what we can do during the weekend. You will start the conversation.

Presentation of Task

Teacher Says in English	**Student Says in English**
I am your friend. We are discussing what we can do during the weekend. You will start the conversation. Do you understand the situation?	Yes, I do.
All right. Remember we'll be discussing what we can do during the weekend. I'll give you a few seconds to think about what you might want to say in Spanish in this situation. (Short pause) Are you ready?	Yes, I am.
From now on, we'll use no more English.	

Task Begins (All in Spanish)

Teacher Says	Student Says	Rating
No quiero ir de compras.	Me gustaría ir de compras.	**1 credit.** Student initiated task. Comprehensible and appropriate.
No puedo comprar nada. No tengo dinero.	¿Por qué? Es divertido y necesito ropa.	**1 credit.** Comprehensible and appropriate.
	Entonces, ¿por qué no vamos al cine? Yo puedo pagar.	**1 credit.** Comprehensible and appropriate.
¿Qué película quieres ver? Me gustan las comedias también.	La comedia nueva en el cine en mi barrio.	**1 credit.** Comprehensible and appropriate.

Quality Point

The Quality Point was earned because:

1. Student had no problem initiating conversation.

2. Student was able to keep the conversation going.

3. Student was able to change the direction of the conversation when necessary.

4. Student needed no second attempt for any utterance.

5. Student used a variety of vocabulary.

6. Student made no structure errors.

Credit for Task: 5 points

Part 1B
Let's Practice!

Socializing

1. I am your friend who is in the hospital. You call to find out how I am. (Student initiates)

2. I am your friend. I ask you what you want to do after school. (Teacher initiates)

3. I am your friend. You call to invite me to dinner. (Student initiates)

4. You are on vacation. You meet me on the beach. I want to find out about you. (Teacher initiates)

5. You are watching television in the evening with a new friend. You are deciding which programs to watch. (Student initiates)

6. We are planning a party together. We discuss whom to invite, what to eat, and other details. (Teacher initiates)

7. I am your friend. We meet at the library, and you want to know more about a student from another school you have seen me with. (Student initiates)

8. I am your mother. Your cousin is coming to visit from Venezuela, and you have never met him. (Teacher initiates)

9. I am a student who has just moved here from Florida. Tell me about your favorite winter sports. (Student initiates)

10. I am your friend from out of town. You have invited me to visit you, and we are talking about our schools. (Teacher initiates)

Providing and Obtaining Information

1. I am your mother. You have just received a birthday gift from your grandparents. Tell me about it. (Student initiates)

2. Your foreign pen pal is coming to visit you this summer. Your friend wants to know what you will do. (Teacher initiates)

3. I am your cousin. I want to arrange a date for you with my friend. Find out about the person. (Student initiates)

4. You have just transferred to a new school. Your friend wants to know all about it. (Teacher initiates)

5. I am the waiter in a restaurant. Give me your breakfast order. (Student initiates)

6. I am your mother. It is Saturday, and I want you to wash the car. You tell me all the things you have to do today. (Teacher initiates)

7. I am the ticket seller at the train station in Madrid. You need to take a train to Bilbao. (Student initiates)

8. I am new in your neighborhood. I need directions to the supermarket. (Teacher initiates)

9. A Costa Rican exchange student sits next to you at lunch in the cafeteria. You ask him/her about life in Costa Rica. (Student initiates)

10. You are at the mall with your aunt, your cousin and your cousin's boy friend. You see a friend, who wants to know what your relationships are. (Teacher initiates)

Expressing Feelings and Opinions

1. I am your teacher and I think you are not enthusiastic about anything. Tell me about your favorite hobbies. (Teacher initiates)

2. I am your friend and I tell you how much I like Math class. You do not like Math class, so explain why. (Student initiates)

3. I am your sister/brother and we are out walking in the winter. I complain about the weather. Tell me why you like the season. (Student initiates)

4. I am a salesclerk trying to sell you something you don't want. Explain why you don't want it. (Teacher initiates)

5. I am your friend, and you tell me about a boy/girl you think you like. (Student initiates)

6. I am a teacher taking a poll about whether students in your school should wear uniforms. Tell me what you think. (Teacher initiates)

7. We are friends in the same class. Our Spanish teacher leaves during the year. Tell me how you feel about the new teacher. (Student initiates)

8. I am your sister/brother. Express your opinion of the new outfit I just bought. (Teacher initiates)

9. I am the manager of the school cafeteria. I am interviewing students about a possible new menu. Tell me your ideas. (Teacher initiates)

10. I am your friend. We are discussing our brothers and sisters. Tell me how you feel about yours. (Student initiates)

Persuasion

1. I am your father/mother. Convince me to let you go to Florida alone to visit your grandparents. (Student initiates)

2. I am your mother. Convince me that you don't feel well and shouldn't go to school. (Student initiates)

3. I am your friend. We can't decide which restaurant to have lunch in. Convince me to go to a particular one. (Teacher initiates)

4. I am your friend. We are shopping and I want you to buy an item of clothing. Convince me it would be better for me. (Teacher initiates)

5. I am your teacher. Convince me it would be a good idea to take a class trip. (Student initiates)

6. I am your parent. I don't want you to have a dog. Convince me to let you get one. (Teacher initiates)

7. Your family is undecided about what to prepare for the evening meal. You have definite ideas about what you would like to eat. (Student initiates)

8. I am your friend, and I don't like exercise. Try to persuade me to get exercise by joining a sports team. (Teacher initiates)

9. I am your mother. Convince me that you shouldn't take your 8-year-old brother to the beach with you. (Student initiates)

10. You are visiting your grandmother. She wants you to stay for dinner. Convince her that you cannot stay. (Teacher initiates)

Part 2 Listening Comprehension

There are three sections of listening comprehension questions:

Part 2A, questions in English based on listening to passages in Spanish,

Part 2B, questions in Spanish based on listening to passages in Spanish, and

Part 2C, choosing the correct picture from a set, based on listening to passages in Spanish.

Part 2A
Listening Comprehension: Questions in English

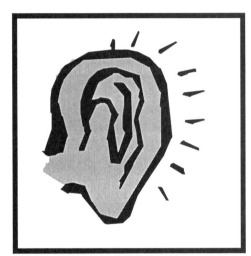

The question

"There are 10 questions in this part. For each question, you will hear some background information in English. Then you will hear a passage in Spanish *twice*, followed by the question in English. Listen carefully. After you have heard the question, read the question and the four suggested answers in your test booklet. Choose the best suggested answer and write its *number* in the appropriate space on your answer sheet." [20 points]

The background

One of the learning outcomes tested on the proficiency exam is your ability to listen to and understand spoken Spanish. On Part 1 you had to *speak* and carry on a conversation. Here you have to *listen* and to answer questions.

Are you a good listener? When people talk to you, can you remember what they said, or were you really thinking about something else? It's important to be able to listen closely without being distracted by other students, thoughts of your next class, or something you see out the window.

You have been studying Spanish all year, listening to your teacher, your friends, and whatever tapes may have been available. If your program has followed the guidelines of the New York State Syllabus, *you will be able to answer this question*. How well you answer it, reflected by your score, will depend on your ability to *listen well*.

The strategy

You can succeed on this part of the examination without understanding every word that you hear. As long as you can pick out *key words* (the words that will provide the key to the information you need) and phrases that are related to the question, you have a good chance of choosing the correct response.

Each passage will be read twice, so you have a second chance to understand what you may have missed on the first reading. The question and choices of answers are in English in this section, so you have somewhat more support than in Part 2B. But remember, you can't just guess at an answer based on the fact that the Spanish wording or vocabulary is similar to what you hear; you do need to understand the meaning of *most* of the listening passage.

What to do at testing time

1. Relax and listen carefully to what is being read. Do not let your thoughts wander or allow anything to distract you.

2. Before you hear the passage for the first time, take a quick look at the question and four possible answers. Now you already have an idea of what to listen for in the passage. Your teacher will read some background information in English. Now you know what the setting or

context of the passage is, so you can be alert for appropriate vocabulary clues in the passage. For an example, take a look at the first question on page 29. The setting is Christmas in Puerto Rico. You may start thinking about Christmas Day, but be careful. Notice that the question asks about the day before Christmas, and how it is celebrated in Puerto Rico. After glancing at the answers, you can start to focus on possible vocabulary in the passage that has to do with *Santa Claus, gifts, festive meal,* and *musical performance.* You don't know yet how this all fits, but you have prepared yourself to hear and analyze certain vocabulary.

3. Listen carefully to the first reading. Even if you hear something unfamiliar, don't worry! Don't get caught up in it! Just relax and do your best to understand the reading. Remember, you already know what it is about, so you are halfway to a correct answer. After this reading, take another quick look at the question and possible answers, taking into account what you have just heard. You may be able to spot some incorrect answers, but don't think about that yet; get ready for the second reading.

4. After the second reading, you will have a little time to respond with the correct answer. First, eliminate the *obviously* wrong answers. Did the passage say anything about gifts? Eliminate answer **b.** Did you hear any reference to a mall? It's true Santa Claus was mentioned, but there was nothing about shopping or the mall. You can safely eliminate answer **a.** Now there are just two to choose from. After the first reading, you understood that going house to house singing is one of the ways Christmas is celebrated. This is not the same as going to a musical performance. Now there is only one choice left, so you know it must be correct, even if you didn't understand every word of the passage.

5. You won't be able to hear the passage a third time, so never go back and change your choice after the second time.

Summary

You may not be *completely* sure of your answer because you did not *fully* understand all of the passage in Spanish. But your ability to listen has combined with your general abilities in Spanish *and your sense of logic*, to move you as close as possible to the correct answer.

Part 2A
Let's Practice!

Listening comprehension passages for this section appear at the end of the section. After listening to each passage twice, circle the letter of the correct choice.

1. You are in Puerto Rico on a student exchange program. You ask your host family about Christmas celebrations on the island and someone tells you:

   How is the evening before Christmas celebrated in Puerto Rico?

   a. going to see Santa Claus at the mall
   b. receiving gifts
   c. having a festive meal
   d. going to a musical performance

2. You have arrived in Spain to visit your pen pal. In the airport a young man approaches you and says:

   Where are Juan's grandparents?

   a. at the airport
   b. in the United States
   c. on a plane
   d. at home

3. You hear this announcement in school:

   What is this announcement about?

   a. a birthday party
   b. a class trip
   c. an end-of-the-year party
   d. a dance

4. You are in a store in the Dominican Republic. The clerk says:

   What kind of food does he sell?

   a. meat
   b. fruit
   c. vegetables
   d. ice cream

5. Your friend is visiting from Puerto Rico and he says:

   What things of interest does the museum have?

   a. Puerto Rican paintings
   b. European art
   c. American crafts
   d. books about artists

6. You are in a department store in Mexico and the clerk says:

   What must you do next?

   a. go to the shoe department
   b. choose another color
   c. pay for the dress
   d. try another size

7. You are invited to your friend's birthday party and you don't know what to get as a gift. Your brother says:

   Where would you go to buy the gift?

   a. clothing store
   b. jewelry store
   c. furniture store
   d. electronics store

8. While traveling in El Salvador you become ill. You go to the doctor and he says:

   What should you do now?

   a. stay in bed
   b. eat normally
   c. go to the hospital
   d. drink a lot of water

9. Your friend is visiting from Ecuador and she says:

   What has your friend never done?

   a. seen snow
   b. watched television
   c. gone ice skating
   d. learned to ski

10. Andres tells the class what he did during his summer vacation.

    What was the weather like during Andres' vacation?

    a. very hot
    b. very cold
    c. cool
    d. raining

11. Your friend calls to see if you can do something together on the weekend. He says:

What does your friend want to do?

- **a.** go to Roberto's house
- **b.** go out in the evening
- **c.** go to the movies
- **d.** go shopping

12. You are in school and hear this announcement:

Who would be interested in this announcement?

- **a.** teachers
- **b.** students who want to play soccer
- **c.** students who want to play in the band
- **d.** parents

13. Your friend is telling you about a special occasion. She says:

What did your friend say about the day?

- **a.** The party was boring.
- **b.** The graduation ceremony lasted a long time.
- **c.** She didn't like the music at the party.
- **d.** The graduation ceremony was in the evening.

14. You are in your Spanish class and the teacher announces:

What is this announcement about?

- **a.** an after-school student activity
- **b.** a Parent-Teachers meeting
- **c.** a student trip
- **d.** a sports event

15. Your friend's family has just bought a new home. He says:

What is your friend's new house like?

   a. small, but nice
   b. located in a noisy neighborhood
   c. painted in two colors
   d. big and roomy

16. You and your friend are talking about school. He says:

What must your friend do?

   a. work on the project tomorrow
   b. hand in the assignment today
   c. write something in Spanish
   d. do an assignment for extra credit

17. While you are in Colombia you hear the weather report on the radio. The announcer says:

What will the weather be like in the afternoon?

   a. cold
   b. sunny
   c. rainy
   d. snowy

18. You are listening to the radio and you hear this announcement:

What is the purpose of this announcement?

   a. to attract patients to a doctor's office
   b. to recruit new doctors
   c. to announce the opening of a new hospital
   d. to sell medicine to patients

19. You are at your cousin's house. He says:

What does your cousin want to do?

   a. go out for lunch
   b. go swimming in the park
   c. take a walk
   d. go skating

20. You are in Nicaragua with your family and you want to go shopping. Your mother says:

Why can't you go shopping?

   a. You only have American currency.
   b. It's too early.
   c. You don't have enough money.
   d. The bank is closed.

21. You are on a trip with your class. Your friend tells you:

What does your friend have to do before returning to school?

   a. go straight home
   b. go to his friend's house
   c. meet his friend
   d. arrange to be picked up

22. Your friend is talking about what he will do during the winter recess. He says:

Where is your friend going during the winter vacation?

   a. a warm place
   b. the mountains
   c. a big city
   d. a beach resort

23. An exchange student from Uruguay is speaking to your class. She says:

How does this student say she feels about her stay in the United States?

   a. She loves to go out and talk to people.
   b. She wants to stay longer.
   c. She misses her country.
   d. She is doing many new things.

24. You are in a restaurant in Bogota. Your friend says:

What does your friend like to order in Hispanic restaurants?

   a. chicken and rice
   b. typical foods of the country
   c. dessert
   d. only beans

25. You are in Mexico and see preparations for a celebration. You ask your friend about it and he says:

What is being celebrated?

   a. a famous battle
   b. a French holiday
   c. Mexico's Mayan heritage
   d. Mexico's independence

Listening Comprehension Passages

1. Como Puerto Rico es parte de los Estados Unidos, hay una celebración que combina la americana de Santa Claus con la fiesta navideña de Puerto Rico. La noche del 24 de diciembre se celebra la Nochebuena con una cena muy grande. Después, vamos de casa en casa cantando y más tarde, vamos a la iglesia.

2. ¡Hola! ¿Es Ud. Pedro? Yo soy Juan. Por favor, venga a conocer a mi familia. Éstos son mi padre Humberto, mi madre Laura y mis hermanos, Francisca, Antonio y Clara. Mis abuelos, María y Carlos, se quedaron en casa.

3. El último día de clases vamos a tener una fiesta en la cafetería. Necesitamos estudiantes y maestros para ayudar con la preparación de esta fiesta. Si está interesado, favor de comunicarse con la secretaria de la escuela lo más pronto posible.

4. Tengo guayabas, mangos, papayas, naranjas, melones, piñas, guanábanas y guineos. Son buenas y baratas. ¿Cuál quiere? Si no conoce las frutas tropicales, compre una guayaba o una guanábana.

5. Vamos a visitar el Museo del Barrio. Dicen que es el mejor museo de pinturas y artesanías puertorriqueñas. Tienen pinturas de los artistas modernos más famosos de la isla. Vale la pena pasar el día allí.

6. Ud. necesita un vestido talla siete, de color azul. No tenemos ningún vestido azul en su talla. Hay otros vestidos en rojo y en amarillo de talla siete.

7. A Miguel le gusta mucho jugar a los juegos de vídeo. Le gustan especialmente los juegos de deportes. ¿Por qué no le compras un juego de béisbol o fútbol americano?

8. No es nada serio. Ud. tiene un virus estomocal. Coma comidas suaves y beba mucho líquido por una semana. Entonces, Ud. va a estar bien y va a poder comer de todo.

9. Por favor, vamos a patinar sobre hielo. Yo nunca he patinado sobre hielo en mi país. Dicen que es muy divertido. Yo he visto personas patinando en el hielo en la tele y no parece ser muy difícil. ¿Cuándo podemos ir?

10. En mis vacaciones de verano, mi familia y yo fuimos a Argentina. A mis padres no les gusta el calor, y por eso, pasamos el verano donde hace mucho frío en el mes de julio.

11. ¿Quieres salir con nosotros? Roberto y yo vamos a ver la nueva película cómica en el centro. Mi primo la vio ayer y le gustó mucho. Vamos a ir el sábado a las dos de la tarde. ¿Puedes venir?

12. El equipo de fútbol necesita más estudiantes este año. Si están interesados, por favor vengan a la oficina del señor Pérez a las cuatro de la tarde.

13. Mi graduación fue ayer en la sala de conferencias de la escuela. La ceremonia fue muy larga y aburrida pero la fiesta fue muy divertida. La música era buena y bailamos toda la noche. Fue la mejor noche de mi vida.

14. Hay una reunión esta tarde a las cuatro para los estudiantes que están interesados en participar en el club de español. Por favor, sean puntuales porque es necesario elegir la junta directiva inmediatamente.

15. La casa está en un barrio tranquilo. Es muy grande y los cuartos son espaciosos. Mi cuarto es hermoso y está pintado de color azul. Tengo un armario muy grande para todas mis cosas. Me encanta mi nueva casa.

16. Yo tengo un proyecto para mi clase de español. Tengo que dárselo a la Sra. López mañana. Tengo que hacer un dibujo además de la parte escrita. Espero terminar el trabajo esta noche.

17. El pronóstico del tiempo para hoy es soleado con lluvias parciales por la tarde. La temperatura ahora es de ochenta grados y bajará a los cincuenta grados por la noche. No hace viento. ¡No olvide llevar su paraguas!

18. Si necesita ayuda médica, venga a la Clínica Diagnóstica Menéndez. La clínica está abierta veinticuatro horas al día. Hay médicos especializados en todas las ramas de la medicina. Estamos aquí para servirles.

19. *¿Quieres ir a patinar? Es peligroso en la calle. ¿Por qué no vamos al parque que está a cinco cuadras de aquí? Tiene un lugar especial para patinar en el medio del parque. Podemos ir después del almuerzo.*

20. *No podemos comprar nada hasta que cambiemos el dinero norteamericano. Tenemos que encontrar un banco para cambiar el dinero a la moneda nicaragüense.*

21. *Por favor, necesito encontrar un teléfono. Tengo que llamar a mis padres. Ellos me dijeron que los llamara antes de regresar a la escuela. Ellos van a recogerme en carro y yo no quiero esperar mucho tiempo.*

22. *Durante las vacaciones de invierno mi hermano y yo vamos a esquiar y a patinar sobre hielo. Nos encantan los deportes del invierno. Sin embargo, a mis padres no les gusta el frío. Ellos van a la Florida donde hace mucho sol y pueden ir a la playa para nadar y tomar el sol.*

23. *Me gusta mucho estar en los Estados Unidos. Sin embargo, en mi país puedo hacer muchas cosas que no puedo hacer aquí. En los Estados Unidos tengo que pasar mucho tiempo en casa porque no sé hablar bien el inglés y tengo miedo de perderme.*

24. *Me gusta mucho la comida hispana. Siempre que voy a un restaurante hispano, como arroz con habichuelas y la carne típica del país. Hoy también voy a comer una arepa, un plato típico colombiano muy sabroso.*

25. *Estamos celebrando el Cinco de Mayo. Muchas personas creen que esta fiesta es el Día de la Independencia de México, pero no lo es; esta fiesta se celebra en septiembre. El Cinco de Mayo celebra una batalla entre los franceses y los mexicanos. Los mexicanos ganaron aunque no tenían tantas armas. Es una celebración de victoria y honra.*

Part 2B
Listening Comprehension: Questions in Spanish

The question

"There are 5 questions in this part. For each question, you will hear some background information in English. Then you will hear a passage in Spanish *twice*, followed by the question in Spanish. Listen carefully. After you have heard the question, read the question and the four suggested answers in your test booklet. Choose the best suggested answer and write its *number* in the appropriate space on your answer sheet." [10 points]

The background

The difference between this part and Part 2A is that the question and answers are in Spanish instead of English. There are also only five questions instead of ten. Now that you have mastered strategies for answering this kind of question, the fact that everything is in Spanish shouldn't be a problem.

The strategy

This is partly a reading as well as a listening test and you should pay attention to the reading element. For Part B, you will be able to look at the question and answers in Spanish while you are listening to the passage. Skim them quickly before the first reading so you are alert to what the passage is about. Now is a time when you can make use of *cognates*, words that sound similar in two different languages, are spelled similarly, and mean roughly the same thing.

The suggestions already given for Part 2A will work for this part as well. You may not have the advantage of completely understanding the question and choice of answers, but even if you don't, you can exercise your logical abilities.

 What to do at testing time

1. It is important to look at the question and answers just before the first reading. Try to understand the key words that make each answer different. For example, in the first practice question on page 41, you see the words "*¿Adónde debes ir . . . ?*" You know that part means "Where must you go . . . ?" Two of the answers contain cognates: *cine* (cinema) in answer **a**, and *farmacia* (pharmacy) in answer **b**. The answers name four different places. That means that the passage must describe something about one of those places. When you hear another cognate, *vitaminas* (vitamins) in the reading, which answer is obviously correct?

2. Be careful when you see the same words in an answer that you hear being read, because this does not always indicate the correct response.

3. You should narrow your choices by the second reading.

4. Be sure to listen to the entire passage before you make your choice. The key to the answer may be in the last sentence.

5. You may need to get to the correct answer through logic rather than facts. For example, the passage may not say it is winter, but if it mentions cold, snow, January, or warm clothing, you can make that connection if the question is "What season is it?"

Part 2B
Let's Practice!

Listening comprehension passages for this section appear at the end of the section. After listening to each passage twice, circle the letter of the correct choice.

1. You are going out with your friends. Your mother says:

   ¿Adónde debes ir antes de volver a casa?

   a. al cine
   b. a la farmacia
   c. a la biblioteca
   d. al correo

2. You hear this announcement on the radio:

   ¿Qué puedes ganar en el concurso?

   a. una cámara
   b. un perro
   c. una invitación a la parada
   d. comida de perro

3. You are staying with your pen pal in Argentina. He says:

   ¿Con quién quiere ir tu amigo a bailar?

   a. con su familia
   b. con sus nuevas amigas
   c. con los músicos
   d. con su novia

4. You are in Peru and need to mail a letter. You ask for directions to the post office and are told:

   ¿Dónde está el correo?

   a. cerca de la parada de autobús
   b. muy lejos
   c. en la esquina
   d. en la calle Río Grande

5. You are in a bank in El Salvador and the teller says:

   ¿Qué dice Ud.?

   a. Está bien. Quiero depositar dinero.
   b. Está bien. Necesito sacar dinero.
   c. Está bien. Quiero cambiar cheques de viajeros.
   d. Está bien. No tengo dólares.

6. You are listening to the radio in Chile and hear the following:

   ¿De qué se trata el programa?

   a. de comedia
   b. de música
   c. de misterio
   d. de drama

7. You and your friend plan on going camping this weekend. Your friend says:

   ¿Por qué no van a poder ir?

   a. No tienen radio.
   b. Va a hacer mal tiempo.
   c. No tienen dinero.
   d. No tienen transporte.

8. You invite your friend to go to the movies with you, but she says:

   ¿Por qué no puede ir al cine tu amiga?

   a. Está visitando a su familia.
   b. Va a una fiesta.
   c. Tiene que estudiar.
   d. Está enferma.

9. Your friend calls you and says:

   ¿Adónde te invita tu amigo?

   a. al parque
   b. a la piscina
   c. al teatro
   d. a la biblioteca

10. Your class is going on a trip. Your teacher says:

    ¿Qué van a hacer los estudiantes?

    a. Van a ir al teatro.
    b. Van a cocinar.
    c. Van a bailar.
    d. Van a comer una comida mexicana.

11. You are an exchange student in Paraguay. Your classmate says to you:

¿Qué van a hacer los amigos esta noche?

    a. Van a una fiesta.
    b. Van al teatro.
    c. Van al centro.
    d. Van al museo.

12. You hear this announcement on the radio in San Juan:

¿Qué se puede comprar en esta tienda?

    a. comida
    b. ropa
    c. muebles
    d. joyas

13. You are staying with a family in Bolivia. Your host parent says to you:

¿Qué información te da el padre?

    a. cómo hacer una llamada telefónica
    b. cómo ir al aeropuerto
    c. cómo viajar en la ciudad
    d. cómo ir al campo

14. You meet a new student in your class who is from Guatemala. He says:

¿Qué necesita el alumno?

    a. ir a la cafetería
    b. hablar con la profesora de inglés
    c. encontrar una librería
    d. obtener información para una clase

15. Your family is planning a vacation. Your father says:

¿Cuánto tiempo quiere el padre pasar en México?

    a. veintiún días
    b. un mes
    c. una semana
    d. catorce días

16. You visit your friend who has not been in school for a few days. He says:

¿Por qué se muda tu amigo?

    a. Su padre tiene un trabajo nuevo.
    b. Él va de vacaciones.
    c. A su familia no le gusta su casa.
    d. Su familia necesita una casa más grande.

17. Your cousin reads you an ad she is considering replying to. She says:

¿Qué le interesa a su prima?

    a. vender su coche
    b. comprar una casa
    c. prepararse para una carrera
    d. encontrar un novio

18. You want to go out with your friend. He says:

¿Qué te pregunta tu amigo?

    a. ¿Qué clase de película quieres ver?
    b. ¿Cuál es tu fiesta favorita?
    c. ¿A qué escuela quieres asistir?
    d. ¿A qué teatro quieres ir?

19. You are shopping with your friend. She says:

¿Qué dice tu amiga de la blusa?

   a. Es de mala calidad.
   b. No le gusta el color.
   c. Cuesta demasiado.
   d. Es fea.

20. You and your friend are talking about your future plans. She says:

¿De qué habla tu amiga?

   a. de dónde quiere vivir en el futuro
   b. de su esposo ideal
   c. de su carrera preferida
   d. de su graduación

Listening Comprehension Passages

1. *Cuando regreses, por favor, tráeme las vitaminas y las aspirinas. No te olvides de recoger la medicina para la garganta.*

2. *Tu perro puede darte un paseo. Nuestra compañía está buscando el perro ideal. Si el tuyo gana, tú y tu perro serán invitados a la parada puertorriqueña. Envía una foto de tu perro y una carta explicando porqué tu perro es ideal.*

3. *¿Quieres ir a bailar este fin de semana? Hay un grupo musical muy bueno en el Club Miramar. La música es fantástica. Podemos invitar a las muchachas que conocimos ayer en el parque.*

4. *El correo está a tres cuadras de aquí. Puedes tomar el autobús o puedes caminar. Si caminas, sigue derecho y entonces dobla a la derecha en la calle Río Grande. El correo está a mitad de la cuadra.*

5. *Para cambiar dinero norteamericano, tiene que mostrarme su pasaporte. El cambio de dinero le va a costar un por ciento de comisión. El cambio está a veinticinco pesos por dólar.*

6. *Atención, señoras y señores. Esta noche el Canal Dos va a presentar un programa especial sobre los cantantes latinoamericanos. Comienza a las ocho de la noche y termina a las once. ¡No se lo pierda!*

7. *No podemos ir al campo. Para el fin de semana anuncian lluvia. Va a llover todo el tiempo. Oí el pronóstico del tiempo esta mañana en la radio.*

8. *Lo siento pero no puedo ir contigo hoy. Tengo un virus, me duele la cabeza y tengo mucha fiebre. El médico me dijo que guardara cama. Tal vez podemos ir al cine la semana que viene.*

9. *Tengo boletos para ver "El Quijote." Dicen que es una obra muy buena. Los actores son excelentes. Se estrena mañana a las dos de la tarde. ¿Quieres ir conmigo?*

10. *Vamos al restaurante "El Sombrero" el miércoles. Vamos a comer tacos, enchiladas, guacamole, arroz con pollo y helado. También hay un programa de bailes mexicanos.*

11. *Esta noche hay una fiesta en la casa de mi amigo. Si quieres, puedes venir con nosotros. Vamos en el carro de Pedro. La fiesta empieza a las nueve.*

12. *Señoras y señores, vengan y visiten nuestra nueva tienda en la calle Verbena en Bayamón. ¡Hay muchas rebajas! Todo lo que Uds. necesitan para amueblar su casa. Hay camas, butacas, sofás, armarios, escritorios y mucho más.*

13. *Cuando quieras ir a algún sitio y nosotros no estemos en casa, puedes tomar el autobús a dos cuadras de la casa. El autobús va al centro, a la biblioteca, al banco y al correo.*

14. *Hace solamente dos meses que estoy en esta escuela. ¿Me puedes ayudar? Tengo que escribir un informe para la clase de inglés y no sé dónde queda la biblioteca pública. Necesito sacar un libro.*

15. *¿Por qué no vamos a México de vacaciones? Me gustaría nadar en las bellas playas de Acapulco. También podemos ir al Parque de Chapultepec en la Ciudad de México para ver el castillo. Podemos quedarnos por tres semanas en México.*

16. *¿Sabes que vamos a mudarnos? Mi padre aceptó un trabajo en otro país. Nosotros tenemos que irnos este fin de semana. Voy a echar de menos a mis amigos.*

17. *Conviértase en profesional de la salud. Tenemos cursos en inglés y en español. Hay clases para asistente médico y técnico en enfermería. Abrimos los siete días de la semana.*

18. *Hoy es un día de fiesta y no tenemos que ir a la escuela. ¿Por qué no vamos al cine cerca de mi casa? Hay varias películas nuevas: una comedia, un drama y una película de aventuras. ¿Qué prefieres?*

19. *Me gusta mucho esta blusa. Está muy de moda y el color rosado es bonito. Es de buena calidad, pero es un poco cara. ¿Tiene Ud. una de rebaja?*

20. *Quiero ser doctora porque me gustaría ayudar a la gente enferma. Quiero asistir a la universidad para estudiar medicina. Tengo que estudiar por muchos años. Me gustaría trabajar en un hospital.*

Part 2C Listening Comprehension with Picture

The question

"There are 5 questions in this part. For each question, you will hear some background information in English. Then you will hear a passage in Spanish *twice*, followed by the question in English. Listen carefully. After you have heard the question, read the question and look at the four pictures in your test booklet. Choose the picture that best answers the question and write its *number* in the appropriate space on your answer sheet." [10 points]

The background

You must listen very carefully in this section, because you won't have the choices of Spanish answers written down to remind you if your mind wanders. There is only one question for each set of four pictures, so you are only listening for one piece of information in the Spanish passage that you will hear.

The strategy

Before you hear the background information in English, read the written question. Then take a quick look at the four pictures. Now you have an idea what information to listen for in the passage, and what words might be the *key* to answering the question. For example, look at practice question 1 on page 51. The question is "Which one is Dolores?" and there are pictures of an old lady, a little girl, a teenager, and a middle-aged lady. Since these people are all different ages, you can guess that the *key word(s)* will be something about age. Now turn to page 57 and read the background and the passage in Spanish.

Remember, you won't have the advantage of seeing the words written down, so you must pay careful attention. The first time you hear the passage, listen for the key word and any words around it that help to explain it. What is in the first sentence of this passage? *Sesenta y cinco años*. That sounds like a lot of years. Maybe Dolores is the old lady. And, yes, the passage tells you next how many children and grandchildren she has. If you weren't listening carefully, you could have missed that first sentence.

Use the second reading of the passage to check the correctness of your choice, and to understand any words you might have missed the first time around.

What to do at testing time

1. Look quickly at the pictures before the passage is read. Try to figure out the context of each picture and pick out the key things you might need to listen for.

2. Look for anything that makes each picture in a set different—males/females, different times of day, weather conditions, settings.

3. Look for similarities and differences that might be confusing. For example, if two pictures have books in them, "book" is probably not the key word. Perhaps it is library, bookstore, reading or studying. Listen for these words in the Spanish passage.

Part 2C
Let's Practice!

Listening comprehension passages for this section appear at the end of the section. After listening to each passage twice, circle the letter of the correct choice.

1. Which one is Dolores?

A

B

C

D

2. What is Juan doing this summer?

A

B

C

D

3. How is Mateo?

  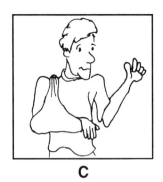 

A   B   C   D

4. Where does Felipe's father go each day?

A   B   C   D

5. What kind of student is Raul?

A   B   C   D

6. What does Ernesto like best?

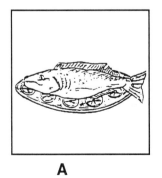   

A   B   C   D

7. What does Mercedes do?

A B C D

8. What does Mrs. Ramos need to buy for the trip?

 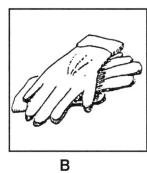  

A B C D

9. How will they get to Carmen's house?

A B C D

10. What would you want to do?

A B C D

11. Where does Luisa go?

A B C D

12. What does Andres want to be?

A B C D

13. What is her uncle like?

A B C D

14. What will the group do this weekend?

A B C D

15. What is your cousin going to do?

A　　　　　　　　B　　　　　　　　C　　　　　　　　D

16. What kind of weather is forecast?

A　　　　　　　　B　　　　　　　　C　　　　　　　　D

17. What is the weather like in Argentina in December?

A　　　　　　　　B　　　　　　　　C　　　　　　　　D

18. What does your friend plan to do?

A　　　　　　　　B　　　　　　　　C　　　　　　　　D

19. Which sport do both boys dislike?

A	B	C	D

20. Where is one place you might go?

A	B	C	D

Listening Comprehension Passages

1. Your father is telling you about a new neighbor. He says:
   Dolores Martín tiene sesenta y cinco años. Su familia es grande. Ella tiene seis hijos y doce nietos. A Dolores y a su esposo Roberto les encanta la visita de sus nietos.

2. Your friend is telling you how her brother will spend his vacation. She says:
   Durante las vacaciones de verano Juan está muy ocupado. Le gustaría viajar pero no puede porque tiene que asistir a la escuela de verano. Después de las clases él trabaja en una tienda porque necesita dinero.

3. You call your friend and his sister tells you:
   Mateo tiene un resfriado y fiebre y no puede asistir a la escuela. El médico le dice que tiene que quedarse en cama por unos días.

4. Felipe is telling you about his father's typical day. He says:
   Todos los días después del trabajo mi padre compra un periódico. Le gusta leer acerca de las noticias del mundo y también acerca de los deportes.

5. Your aunt is asking you to help your cousin in school. She says:
   Raúl no es un buen estudiante en la clase de español. No estudia mucho y habla poco en la clase. No contesta las preguntas y saca malas notas en los exámenes.

6. You invited Ernesto to dinner and his mother tells you:
   A Ernesto le gusta comer. Come muchas legumbres con carne o pescado, pero su parte favorita de la comida es el postre.

7. Mercedes' brother is telling you how she tries to stay well. He says:
   Para mantenerse de buena salud Mercedes hace varias cosas. Toma vitaminas, hace ejercicios, come bien y visita regularmente al médico.

8. Your mother tells you about her friend's family's plans. She says:
   La familia Ramos va a la costa para pasar las vacaciones. A todos los miembros de la familia les gusta la playa y piensan pasar mucho tiempo tomando el sol y nadando.

9. Carolina tells you about something she wants to do on vacation. She says:
Mi esposo y yo recibimos instrucciones para llegar a la casa de Carmen. La casa no está muy lejos del hotel. Nosotros decidimos caminar porque hace buen tiempo.

10. You hear this weather forecast on the radio:
Hoy está nublado. Hay posibilidad de lluvias y la humedad está al cien por ciento. La temperatura será de setenta grados todo el día.

11. Luisa is telling you what she does in the summer. She says:
Cuando hace mucho calor y la temperatura está en los noventa grados, me gusta pasar el día al aire libre. Voy a un lugar donde hace más fresco y puedo tomar el sol.

12. Your friend tells you about his brother's career plans. He says:
Andrés quiere trabajar en un restaurante. Le gusta cocinar en casa y muchas veces ayuda a mi madre a preparar la comida.

13. Your friend is describing her uncle to you. She says:
Mi tío Pedro es un hombre muy distinguido. Él se viste muy bien. Es hombre de negocios y tiene bastante dinero.

14. You are visiting your pen pal in Spain and she invites you to go out with a group of her friends. She says:
Mis amigos y yo siempre salimos durante los fines de semana. Algunas veces vamos a las cafeterías o a las discotecas, pero este sábado queremos ir al cine.

15. Your cousin calls to tell you some exciting news. She says:
Voy a hacer un viaje a Puerto Rico. Voy con un grupo de estudiantes de mi escuela. Es un programa de intercambio para el verano. Me puedes escribir a esta dirección: Calle Miramar, número 23, Río Piedras, Puerto Rico 09030.

16. You are in the Dominican Republic and hear this announcement on the radio:
¡Aviso sobre el tiempo! El Huracán Andrés se acerca a la isla. Habrá vientos fuertes y lluvias. Por favor, tomen medidas de precaución. Cubran las ventanas con madera y tengan agua y comida enlatada suficientes para una semana.

17. Your friend calls you to talk about his vacation. He says:
Mi familia y yo vamos a la Argentina en diciembre para pasar las vacaciones. Aunque es invierno aquí, en la Argentina es verano y podemos nadar.

18. You call your friend to invite him to a party. He says:
Lo siento pero pasé todo el día en el parque y estoy muy cansado. Montamos en bicicleta, patinamos y jugamos al baloncesto. Ahora quiero acostarme.

19. Your brother is telling you about the sports he and his friend like. He says:
Nos gusta jugar a muchos deportes. El béisbol, el fútbol y el baloncesto son nuestros favoritos. También nos gustan el tenis y el fútbol americano. El que no nos gusta es el hockey, porque ese deporte es muy peligroso.

20. You are in Madrid and ask your guide for suggestions for places to go during the weekend. He says:
Hay una película muy buena en el Cine Lope de Vega. También hay una obra dramática en el Teatro Calderón. Si prefiere otras actividades, puede ir a un partido de fútbol o a una corrida de toros.

Part 3 Reading Comprehension

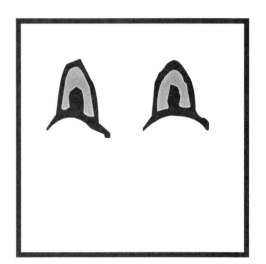

There are three sections of reading comprehension questions:

Part 3A, questions in English based on examples of authentic materials,

Part 3B, questions in Spanish based on examples of authentic materials, and

Part 3C, one topical passage with questions in English.

Part 3A
Reading Authentic Materials: Questions in English

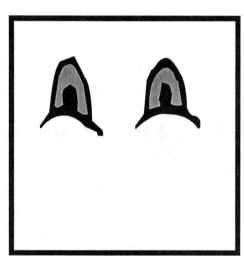

The question

"There are 3 questions in this part. For each, you must answer a question in English based on a reading selection in Spanish. Choose the best answer to each question and write its *number* in the appropriate space on your answer sheet." [6 points]

The background

The authentic materials you will be reading include things like newspaper advertisements, invitations and brochures. You may not understand every word in each piece presented. Don't worry about that. The question has been chosen so that to answer it you only need to know certain vocabulary and structures appropriate to your first year of study.

The strategy

These short reading selections are just like items you read in English all the time. Headlines draw your attention; lists of items will sum up points; what an ad looks like will often be familiar. Beware of jumping to conclusions! Often the word or contextual clue (something about the setting) that draws your attention in a brief passage can be misleading. Advertising copywriters often make "shocking statements" to attract your attention.

In some cases you might be tempted to eliminate a portion of an ad or short reading because it seems unrelated to the question. This can be helpful in narrowing your path to the correct answer. But be careful when you do this! Advertisements in particular are cleverly written.

What to do at testing time

1. Look at the question first. The choices of answers may have two that are similar, but there will be differences among the four. Once you know what you are looking for, it will be much easier to read the sample passage with a specific purpose.

2. Make use of cognates (words that sound the same and mean the same thing in different languages). For example, an ad for a school that teaches English might say *precio razonable* and the question might refer to an advantage of the school. Being able to recognize "reasonable price" can help you find the answer.

3. The same is true for illustrations. Say an ad for a restaurant says *marisquería* and has a picture of a lobster. That would help in answering the question, "What is the specialty of this restaurant?"

4. Check for vocabulary clues. For example, if you had to match a weather report with an appropriate activity, look for the parts of the report that would go with each choice. If skiing was one of the answer choices but the report said sunny and hot, it obviously would be the wrong answer.

5. Read over the entire sample. You can't know in advance where the clues you need will be found.

6. Be careful of false cognates and similar wording in the sample and any answer.

7. An ad for a beauty salon mentions *bodas-cumpleaños*. For the question, "Why would someone go here?" one answer choice is "to buy a wedding

dress." It's wrong, but you might choose it over "to get a haircut," if you are basing your answer on the one word "*boda*" (wedding).

Watch for vocabulary that may be misleading. A contest entry blank says, *No es necesario comprar para participar,* and also has the line, *Yo compro mis productos Pepsi en* ____. You'll have to read the question carefully to see which fact is applicable to choosing the correct answer.

8. Questions may also be stated in negative form. What's not there may be as important as what is. An ad for a shoe store may give several advantages to shopping there. The choices of answers might include "large selection," "lowest prices," "latest styles," and "open every day." But if the question were "What is not mentioned in the ad?" you would have to look for the choice that *isn't* in the ad.

9. Take your time and if you have to guess, make it a logical guess rather than a wild one.

Part 3A
Let's Practice!

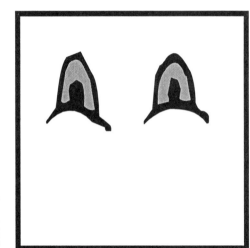

Directions: Circle the letter of your answer choice.

Aplícate el protector de 20 a 30 minutos antes de salir de la casa para que los ingredientes tengan tiempo de actuar. Reaplícalo cada dos o tres horas o más, si nadas o sudas mucho. No importa que la etiqueta diga que es a prueba de agua o de sudor. Evita acostarte sobre la arena, ésta llega a absorber el producto. Pon en vez, una toalla.

1. Who is this advice intended for?

   a. someone going to the beach
   b. someone going to the movies
   c. someone going to school
   d. someone going shopping

2. What can you find on this website?

   a. recipes for fast foods
   b. location of fast food restaurants
   c. fast food menus
   d. health value of fast foods

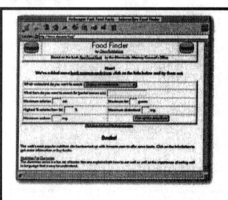

www.olen.com/food
Si te encanta la comida rápida, consulta esta página y encontrarás la tabla de nutrientes completa de cada especialidad. McDonald's, Domino's Pizza y Taco Bell son sólo algunos famosos restauranteros que navegan por este sitio.

ACUARIO
20 de enero - 18 de febrero

Entierra preocupaciones ya que es tiempo de que te relajes y disfrutes de esos momentos tan agradables dentro de tu círculo familiar. Tu relación con tus padres se enfatiza favorablemente. Gustarás de hacer cambios en tu hogar como decorar, renovar el jardín, o hacer mejoras. Tu sentido del gusto se exalta.
Números de suerte: 21, 36, 3.

3. What is the focus of this horoscope?

   a. money
   b. home and family
   c. love
   d. travel

HOY
Aumento de la nubosidad

Se acerca por la mitad occidental un frente frío que producirá un aumento de la nubosidad en zonas del oeste y del norte de la Península. Además, durante la tarde habrá condiciones favorables para que las nubes se desarrollen y se originen fenómenos tormentosos en zonas montañosas del interior y en puntos de Navarra, Aragón, La Rioja y Cataluña. También en el sur del Mediterráneo la nubosidad será abundante, especialmente durante las primeras horas.

4. What kind of weather will most places have?

a. cold
b. sunny
c. foggy
d. cloudy

5. What is this offer?

a. to buy a new book
b. to buy records
c. to receive a free newspaper
d. to subscribe to a magazine

6. Who would be interested in this ad?

a. someone who wants to buy clothing
b. someone who wants to furnish a house
c. someone who wants to take a trip
d. someone who wants to eat in a restaurant

Aquí todos juegan

Si lo que buscas es un deporte en el que puedas ejercitar todo el cuerpo, el basquet es lo tuyo, pues a la hora del juego intervienen todos los músculos, desde las piernas y abdomen, hasta pecho, cuello y brazos. Todos trabajan al máximo no sólo en los partidos, sino en cada entrenamiento, que dura aproximadamente ¡dos horas!

7. What does it say about basketball?

a. It's good exercise.
b. It's fun.
c. It's difficult to learn to play.
d. You must be tall to play.

---

8. What special feature of the trip is highlighted in this ad?

a. It's faster than others.
b. There is service every day.
c. You can take your car on the ship.
d. The fare is inexpensive.

Por mar el viaje es otra cosa.
(para tu coche también)

Una nueva vía nace entre **España e Italia**. Tiene el azul del mar y de Grandi Navi Veloci. Ven a recorrerla, así tu coche disfrutará también del viaje. A bordo del **Fantastic** te esperan **cabinas de lujo con servicios privados, restaurantes a la carta, cafeteria, bar, salones de fiestas, casino, discoteca, cine, piscina, centro fitness y centro shopping**. Y cuando llegues a Génova, puedes seguir hacia Cerdeña o Sicilia a bordo de **Excellent, Excelsior, Majestic, Spendid** y **Victory**. ¿Conoces un modo más agradable de empezar las vacaciones?

¡CAMPEONES DE LIGA!

TODOS ELLOS FORMAN PARTE DE LA SOCIEDAD DE DEBATES DEL CENTRO UNIVERSITARIO FRANCISCO DE VITORIA, UNA INICIATIVA DE PREPARACIÓN CULTURAL Y PROFESIONAL.

EL CENTRO UNIVERSITARIO FRANCISCO DE VITORIA FELICITA A SUS ALUMNOS DE LAS FACULTADES DE DERECHO, Y CIENCIAS ECONÓMICAS Y EMPRESARIALES, **CAMPEONES DE LA PRIMERA LIGA NACIONAL DE DEBATE UNIVERSITARIO**

FRANCISCO DE VITORIA

9. What did the students do?

a. They won an academic competition.
b. They won a soccer championship.
c. They graduated from college.
d. They became scientists.

10. When would this advice apply?

a. when you leave on vacation
b. when there's an emergency
c. when you don't feel well
d. when a salesman calls

CONSEJOS ÚTILES PARA ESCAPAR DEL FUEGO

- Planee Dos Salidas
- Manténgase Calmado
- Cierre Las Puertas
- NO VUELVA A ENTRAR POR NINGUNA RAZÓN

11. Why would someone use this coupon?

a. to place an ad
b. to answer an ad
c. to subscribe to the newspaper
d. to apply for a job

12. What kind of document is this?

a. student ID
b. driver's license
c. passport
d. work ID

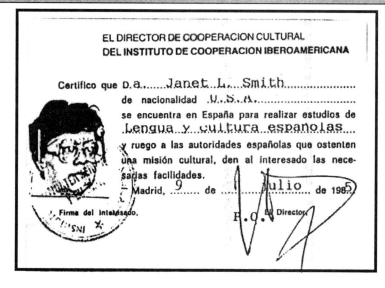

Parque Rómulo Betancourt: *Es un lugar muy interesante donde encontrará una serie de actividades para su distracción: Un planetario, lago artificial con lanchas de remos y una réplica de La Santa María (carabela con que Cristóbal Colón descubrió América), Zoológico con fauna nacional y restaurantes. Cerrado los lunes.*

13. According to this description, what can you do in the park?

a. ice skate
b. swim
c. go to a concert
d. see animals

14. Who would be interested in this ad?

a. someone who wants to buy clothing
b. someone who wants to furnish a home
c. someone who wants to eat out
d. someone who wants to sell a home

DIA 1.º COSTA DEL SOL - BAEZA - UBEDA - CAZORLA

Salida a la hora prevista en dirección a BAEZA con una corta visita panorámica de esta ciudad. Continuación hasta UBEDA: **Almuerzo en Restaurante** y tiempo libre para visita.

Salida hacia CAZORLA: Llegada y traslado al Hotel. Resto del día a disposición. **Cena y Alojamiento.**

DIA 2.º CAZORLA - SIERRA DE CAZORLA - COSTA DEL SOL

Desayuno en el Hotel y salida hacia el Parque Nacional de Cazorla, donde visitaremos el Mirador del Valle, el Parque Cinegético, el Museo de la Torre del Vinagre, la Piscifactoría y el Embalse del Tranco, formando todo ello parte de un paisaje maravilloso que hace de la Sierra de Cazorla la principal reserva forestal de Andalucía.

Regreso al Hotel y **Almuerzo.** Por la tarde salida hacia la Costa del Sol. Llegada y fin de nuestros servicios.

15. How many meals are included on the tour?

a. 4
b. 3
c. 5
d. none

Part 3B
Reading Authentic Materials: Questions in Spanish

The question

"There are 3 questions in this part. For each, you must answer a question in Spanish based on a reading selection in Spanish. Choose the best answer to each question and write its *number* in the appropriate space on your answer sheet." [6 points]

The background

The difference between this section and Section 3A is that the questions and answers are in Spanish. Now that you've mastered the strategies presented in Part 3A, you should do fine with the Spanish selections.

The strategy

Just as in Part 2B, the section with questions and answers in Spanish can present a challenge. However, unlike the listening comprehension, you can read the samples and the question and answers as many times as necessary before choosing (within the time limits of the test).

Part 3B
Let's Practice!

Directions: Circle the letter of your answer choice.

para caballeros y niños

25%-40% de descuento en los trajes de vestir de diseño
Ahorros de los precios regulares en los modelos americanos y europeos, y de nuestro exclusivo Joseph & Lyman y Metropolitan View.

29.99 camisas de campo y pantalones khaki
A su elección de Est Island. Reg. 38.00-45.00

19.99-29.99 camisas stretch y tees mercerizados
Selección de una gran variedad de Joseph & Lyman y de East Island.
Reg. 24.00-34.00

30% de descuento en los sacos deportivos de primavera y pantalones de vestir
Ahorros de los precios originales en nuestra colección completa de Metropolitan View y Joseph & Lyman.

1. ¿Qué está de rebaja?

a. la ropa
b. la comida
c. los muebles
d. los juguetes

MARBELLA. Piso de lujo a estrenar, 206 metros cuadrados, totalmente equipado, tres dormitorios más servicio, cuatro baños, dos plazas de garaje, todo ello en residencial de 24 viviendas pensadas para altos ejecutivos. Precio 48.000.000 pesetas. Teléfono 606961975.

2. ¿A quiénes les interesa este anuncio?

a. a los que quieren viajar
b. a los que quieren empleo
c. a los que quieren comprar una casa
d. a los que quieren comprar un coche

3. ¿Qué pueden hacer los participantes en el concurso?
a. conocer a un atleta
b. ir a un partido de béisbol
c. jugar al béisbol
d. ganar dinero

TELEMADRID

7.30 A saber.
8.00 Cyberclub.
9.30 Buenos días, Madrid.
12.15 Bonanza.
13.05 La niñera.
13.30 Telenoticias 13.30.
14.00 Telenoticias.
15.30 Con T de tarde.
17.50 Adivina, adivinanza.
18.50 Madrid directo.
20.30 Telenoticias.
21.35 Macumba Te Ve.
    Presentan Víctor
    Sandoval y Francine
    Gálvez.
23.45 Max madera.
    Concurso de cine
    presentado por
    Antonio Albert.
1.05 Posiblemente el mejor
    cine del siglo. «Una
    noche en
    Casablanca». USA.
    1946. 83 min. Dir:
    Archie Mayo. Int: Los
    Hermanos Marx.
2.45 Telenoticias.
3.00 Documental.
    «Picapiedra: Lo mejor
    de Piedradura».
3.50 Documental.
    «Mediterráneo».

4. ¿A qué hora puede ver una película?

a. 9:30
b. 14:00
c. 18:50
d. 1:05

5. ¿Cuántos cuartos tiene la casa?

a. 2
b. 7
c. 6
d. 8

702 FLORIDA VENTAS DIVERSA

Casa en 80 x 120' lote, 2 dorms
2 baños. Garaje. Comedor completo.
Sala, cocina. Precio $79.900.00!!
Llame 1-800-649-1134
FLORIDA PROPERTIES

PERU

Flor de María Virginia
19 años
Urb. Corima Mz A1, Lt50,
Calle Magisterio #15,
La Molina, Lima, Perú.
Pasatiempos: dibujar, escribir cartas, leer, salir con mis amigos, coleccionar todo sobre Brad Pitt y ver películas.

6. ¿Qué le gusta hacer a Flor?

a. ir al cine
b. mirar la televisión
c. bailar
d. cocinar

PANADERIA Y REPOSTERIA EL DORADO
EN PUERTO PLATA
HIGIENE Y CALIDAD
ESPECIALIDAD EN TODO TIPO DE PAN, GALLETAS Y DULCES
586-3707
SAN FELIPE 34
PUERTO PLATA

7. ¿Qué se vende en esta tienda?

a. postres
b. ropa
c. muebles
d. frutas y legumbres

---

8. ¿Qué sitio es?

a. rascacielos
b. parque
c. museo
d. teatro

> Este importante complejo de edificios comerciales y financieros, incluye entre otros a las mundialmente conocidas Torres Gemelas de 110 pisos de altura; fueron diseñadas por el arquitecto Minoru Yamasaki; se empezaron a construir en 1966 y se inauguraron en 1970. En la torre número 2, se encuentra localizado el observatorio, desde donde se divisa una increíble panorámica.

IDIOMA

El idioma oficial es el inglés. Debido a que New York es una ciudad tan cosmopolita por la diversidad de su población, es normal oír hablar diferentes idiomas y dialectos. El español es el segundo de más importancia; es fácil encontrar ayuda e información, puesto que la población hispanoparlante supera los dos millones.

9. ¿Qué dice este párrafo?

a. En NY la gente habla solamente inglés.
b. En NY la gente habla solamente español.
c. En NY la gente habla muchas lenguas diferentes.
d. En NY nadie habla español.

ANTIGUA TABERNITA

LA BOLA

Casa fundada en 1870

Cocina casera
Especialidad cocido a la madrileña (puchero barro individual)
Platos regionales

Bola, 5 - MADRID - Tel. 247 69 30
Dirección: WAMBA
Torija, 7 - MADRID-13
Teléfs. 247 15 02 - 248 51 35

10. ¿Para quién es importante este anuncio?

a. para una persona que le gusta comer
b. para una persona que le gusta leer
c. para una persona que le gusta bailar
d. para una persona que le gusta ir al cine

ENTRENESE

PARA UN BUEN TRABAJO EN MENOS DE 6 MESES

- AGENTE DE VIAJES
- COMPUTADORAS
- "DATA ENTRY"
- ASISTENTE DENTAL
- ENFERMERIA AUXILIAR
- ELECTROCARDIOGRAFIA
- TECNICA DENTAL
- INGLES y Equivalente de E.S.

Clases días, noches y sábados
Ayuda Financiera (Si Califica)

TTC
101 W. 31st St. (piso 4)
New York, N.Y.
695-1818

11. Este anuncio ayuda a las personas que quieren

a. aprender algo nuevo.
b. ir al dentista.
c. hacer un viaje.
d. comprar una computadora.

FECHA 31.3.88 HORA 11,40
PARA Teresa Varela
☐ HA VENIDO
☒ HA TELEFONEADO
EL SR. Angela
DE Coruña
TELEFONO
DOMICILIO
ASUNTO Hasta 13'00 estará en casa
NOTA TOMADA POR Miguel

12. ¿Quién llamó?

a. Teresa
b. Coruña
c. Ángela
d. Miguel

13. Este anuncio ofrece:

a. una pastilla de jabón sin pagar
b. un descuento en el futuro
c. una garantía de satisfacción
d. dinero efectivo

14. ¿Qué sugiere este anuncio?

a. Bote los periódicos.
b. Compre algo nuevo.
c. Venda lo que no quiere.
d. Gane cinco dólares.

No hay recogida de objetos reciclables en días festivos o en días de emergencia por nevadas. Si usted recicla **todas las semanas**, coloque los artículos reciclables para su recogida **la semana siguiente**. Si usted recicla **cada *dos* semanas**, coloque los artículos reciclables para su recogida **al día siguiente**.

15. Según esta información, ¿cuándo no debe poner la gente los reciclables?

a. en los fines de semana
b. cuando está lloviendo
c. cuando tiene mucha basura
d. en días de fiesta

Part 3C
Reading a Topical Passage

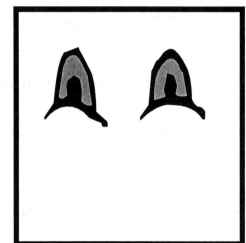

 The question

Part 3C consists of four topical passages in Spanish. For each passage, there is a brief introduction in English followed by the reading passage in Spanish. After each Spanish passage, there are four questions in English. Read each passage in Spanish carefully and then answer each question *in English*. You do not have to answer in a complete sentence. [8 points]

 The background

Part 3C, reading a topical passage, is less difficult than it may seem, because the questions are in English and you will answer them in English. However, you still must read carefully and completely before writing your answer. For example, if a question asks about the color of something, make sure you don't write the first color you see without checking to see if it refers to the item asked about.

The strategy

The introduction in English will tell you the context of the Spanish passage. First read the introduction, then skip down to the questions in English and read them. Now you know what information you are looking for.

Read the complete passage first for basic understanding, then look at the questions again. Read the passage a second time looking for the answer to one question at a time. When you have answered all four questions, go over the passage again to check your answers.

 What to do at testing time

1. The questions often fall in the order that the information is presented in the passage, making it easier to spot the answer. These are not multiple choice questions, so the correct answer isn't there simply to be chosen. You must write the answer yourself. However, remember that you don't have to answer in a complete sentence.

2. Read the questions carefully. Be sure you understand what is being asked. "When is the party?" isn't the same as "Where is the party?" so just finding the word for party won't be enough.

Part 3C
Let's Practice!

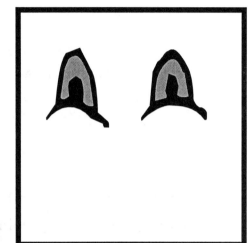

Directions: Write your answer on the line following the question.

1. The following is a composition Roberto wrote.

   Me llamo Roberto Salinas. Asisto a la escuela secundaria. Mi clase favorita es la ciencia. Me gusta mucho porque es una clase muy interesante e informativa.

   Mi profesor es el Sr. Smith. Es inteligente, divertido y simpático. En la clase hacemos muchos experimentos, aprendemos de científicos famosos y tomamos exámenes.

   Para mí la clase es fácil y saco buenas notas.

   Answer the questions in ENGLISH based on the reading.
   1. Which class does Roberto like most? _____
   2. Why does Roberto like the class? _____
   3. How does he describe his teacher? _____
   4. Name one thing he does in class. _____

2. Ana is on vacation and writes to her friend.

Estoy pasándolo muy bien aquí en Acapulco. Es una ciudad muy bonita y divertida. Hace sol y calor y mi familia y yo vamos a la playa todos los días por la mañana. Por la tarde me gusta ir de compras. Hay muchas tiendas que venden ropa y recuerdos de México.

La comida es buena y los mexicanos son simpáticos. Puedo practicar el español con ellos.

Vuelvo a casa la semana que viene.

Ana

Answer the questions in ENGLISH based on the reading.
1. Where is Ana spending her vacation? _____
2. How is the weather? _____
3. Name one activity she does on her trip. _____
4. When is Ana returning home? _____

---

3. Monica received this letter from her pen pal in Costa Rica.

¡Hola! Espero que esta carta te encuentre de buena salud. Yo pienso viajar a los Estados Unidos para pasar un mes en el verano. Me gustaría pasar algunos días con tu familia. Podemos visitar los sitios de interés de la ciudad o ir a la playa o de compras.

Escríbeme y dime la mejor fecha para mi visita. Espero tu carta.

Ángela

Answer the questions in ENGLISH based on the reading.
1. How long will Angela be in the United States? _____
2. Why is she writing to Monica? _____
3. Name an activity that Angela wants to do on her trip. _____
4. What does she want Monica to tell her? _____

4. The following story is about two classmates.

Pedro y Carlos son amigos. Frecuentemente Pedro va a la casa de su amigo después de las clases. Los dos estudian, juegan al baloncesto y miran la televisión.

Carlos invita a Pedro a su casa para cenar los viernes. La madre de Carlos cocina muy bien. Pedro siempre va porque le gusta mucho lo que prepara la madre de su amigo—la comida típica puertorriqueña: arroz con gandules, pernil asado, tostones, y para postre, flan.

Answer the questions in ENGLISH based on the reading.
1. Where does Pedro often go after school? _____
2. Name one activity the friends do together. _____
3. When does Pedro sometimes eat at his friend's house? _____
4. What does Pedro like to eat there? _____

5. Mr. Garcia, from Argentina, writes a letter to his children.

Estoy en los Estados Unidos. Voy a pasar dos semanas aquí. Estoy visitando a mi amigo y su familia. Uno de los hijos de la familia tiene catorce años y está en el primer año de español. Él trata de hablar conmigo porque quiere practicar el idioma. No es fácil porque yo no hablo mucho inglés y hace sólo tres meses que el muchacho estudia el español.

Answer the questions in ENGLISH based on the reading.
1. How long is Mr. Garcia's trip? _____
2. Who is Mr. Garcia visiting? _____
3. Why does one of the children want to speak with him? _____
4. What makes conversation difficult? _____

6. Juan writes about his typical day.

Salgo de la casa a las ocho de la mañana. A las ocho y cuarto pasa el autobús y llego a la escuela a las ocho y media. Por las mañanas tengo cuatro clases. Tomo el almuerzo en la cafetería a las doce. Después del almuerzo tengo tres clases y salgo de la escuela a las tres. Por las tardes juego con mis amigos y hago la tarea. A las seis mis padres, mi hermana y yo tomamos la cena.

Answer the questions in ENGLISH based on the reading.

1. How does Juan travel to school? _____
2. Where does he eat lunch? _____
3. Name an activity Juan does after school. _____
4. When does Juan eat dinner? _____

7. Ricardo writes about his family.

Me llamo Ricardo Vega. Mi familia es grande. Somos mis padres, mi hermana mayor, mi hermano menor y yo. Mi padre se llama Diego y tiene cincuenta años. Él es de México. Mi madre Ana tiene cuarenta y ocho años y es mexicana también. Mi hermana Rosa tiene veintidós años y es maestra. Mi hermano José asiste a la escuela secundaria y tiene quince años. Yo tengo diecinueve años.

Answer the questions in ENGLISH based on the reading.

1. How many people are in Ricardo's family? _____
2. Who is from Mexico? _____
3. What job does Ricardo's sister have? _____
4. How old is Ricardo? _____

8. Carmen is sending this invitation to her friends.

Te invito a una fiesta para celebrar mi graduación de la escuela intermedia. La fiesta es el sábado, el 25 de junio, a las cinco de la tarde en mi casa. Mi dirección es Calle 145, número 320.

Vamos a servir hamburguesas, perros calientes, ensalada, frutas, bebidas, helado y una torta.

Llámame si puedes venir. Mi número es 631-4789.

Carmen

Answer the questions in ENGLISH based on the reading.

1. Why is Carmen having a party? _____
2. Where is the party? _____
3. Name one thing that will be served at the party. _____
4. How should the person let Carmen know if s/he will come? _____

9. Susana writes this letter to a Mexican teen magazine.

Me llamo Susana. Tengo trece años. Tengo el pelo rubio y los ojos azules. Vivo en Los Ángeles, California. Mis clases favoritas son las matemáticas y el arte. Juego al tenis y al baloncesto con mis amigas. Toco la guitarra y canto. También me gusta viajar y me gustaría recibir cartas de jóvenes de otros países. Escríbeme.

Answer the questions in ENGLISH based on the reading.

1. How does Susana describe herself? _____
2. What are Susana's favorite subjects? _____
3. Name one activity she does outside of school. _____
4. Why is she writing this letter? _____

10. Your friend has written these directions for you to get to his house from school.

> *Puedes caminar o puedes tomar el autobús en la esquina de la Calle Washington cerca de la escuela. El autobús va a cruzar el parque. Baja del autobús en la tercera parada, la Avenida Norte. Dobla a la izquierda y camina dos cuadras hasta llegar a la iglesia. Dobla a la derecha y allí en el edificio blanco al lado del restaurante francés es donde yo vivo. Mi dirección es Calle Madison, número 250, décimo piso.*

Answer the questions in ENGLISH based on the reading.
1. What is one way your friend says you can travel? _____
2. Where is the bus stop? _____
3. Name one place near where your friend lives. _____
4. On what floor does your friend live? _____

11. The following is a note Miguel wrote.

> *Queridos abuelos:*
>
> *Muchas gracias por el regalo. Es muy bonito. Voy a poner el televisor en mi dormitorio. Puedo mirar la tele todas las noches después de terminar mis tareas. Durante el fin de semana me gusta mirar los deportes.*

Answer the questions in ENGLISH based on the reading.
1. Whom is Miguel writing to? _____
2. Why is he writing this note? _____
3. Where will he keep his present? _____
4. When will he watch TV? _____

12. The following is from a letter David wrote to his parents.

Me gusta mucho asistir a la escuela aquí en España. Tengo que hablar siempre el español y es una buena manera para aprender la lengua. Ahora hablo y escribo muy bien el castellano.

Voy a los partidos de fútbol y a los museos con mis amigos de clase. También visitamos otros sitios de interés en Madrid. La escuela tiene excursiones a otras ciudades cerca de la capital.

Answer the questions in ENGLISH based on the reading.
1. Why is David in Spain? _____
2. How does he communicate in Spanish now? _____
3. Where does he go with his classmates? _____
4. Name one other thing he does in his free time. _____

13. Pablo wrote this note to his friend.

Estoy enfermo. Tengo un resfriado y fiebre y no puedo ir a la escuela esta semana. ¿Puedes conseguirme la tarea de español? También necesito saber lo que están haciendo en las clases de matemáticas y ciencia.

Voy a llamarte mañana para obtener la información. Muchas gracias por tu ayuda.

Answer the questions in ENGLISH based on the reading.
1. Why isn't Pablo in school? _____
2. What does he need from his friend? _____
3. Name one class he's concerned about. _____
4. When will he call his friend? _____

14. Maria has recently moved and is writing her friend to tell her about her new neighborhood.

Mi barrio es muy bonito y tranquilo. Hay casas grandes y pequeñas, pero no hay edificios de apartamentos. Todas las casas tienen jardines con árboles y flores.

Hay un parque no muy lejos de mi casa. Puedo jugar al baloncesto, patinar y montar en bicicleta allí. La escuela intermedia está frente al parque.

Tenemos que ir en coche o en autobús al cine, al supermercado y a las tiendas.

Answer the questions in ENGLISH based on the reading.
1. How does Maria describe her neighborhood? _____
2. What do all the houses have? _____
3. Where can Maria play near her house? _____
4. Name one place she can't walk to. _____

15. Silvia writes to her aunt to invite her to go shopping.

¿Te gustaría ir de compras conmigo? El cumpleaños de mi madre es el mes que viene y necesito comprarle un regalo.

Podemos ir después de las clases o durante el fin de semana. Me gusta comprar la ropa en las tiendas grandes del centro porque la ropa no es cara y hay un buen surtido. Además, a menudo hay rebajas. ¿Puedes llevarme en tu coche?

Answer the questions in ENGLISH based on the reading.
1. Why does Silvia need to go shopping? _____
2. When does she suggest going? _____
3. Name one reason she likes to shop downtown. _____
4. How will they get to the stores? _____

Part 4 Writing

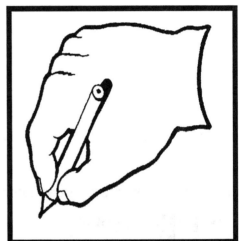

There is one section of writing questions, containing two writing tasks. Both are scored with a set of guidelines that you will want to know about.

Part 4 Writing

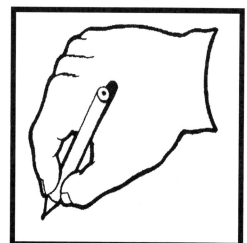

 The question

"In the spaces provided, complete the following *writing task*. This *writing task* should be written entirely in **Spanish** and should contain a minimum of **30** words. Names of people **do not count**. Be sure that you satisfy the purpose of the task. The sentence structure or expressions should be connected logically and should demonstrate a wide range of vocabulary." [5 points]

Note: Part 4 consists of *two* writing tasks. They are very similar, and each one is worth 5 points toward your total score.

 The background

For this part of the examination, you will have to write two notes of 30 words each in Spanish. Your writing ability will be tested in several areas. First and most important is your ability to satisfy the purpose of the task presented. All the sentences you write must be directly related to the task. For example, if the task is to write a note thanking someone for a gift you received, it won't improve your score to include a sentence about the movie you saw last night. If you fail to write at least one sentence related to the task, your entire response will receive a zero, regardless of its other merits.

The two other most important points related to satisfying the purpose of the task are that your writing must be logical and in the correct sequence.

The other aspects of the response that receive separate consideration are your use of vocabulary and structure, and the number of words you use. All of these elements are listed in a set of guidelines that your teacher will use in scoring your writing. Since your work will be compared point by point to this objective scoring standard, you should become familiar with the checklist that the teacher will use.

The actual writing tasks must be written entirely in Spanish and must contain a minimum of 30 words each to get full credit. There are guidelines for which words are allowable to count in the 30. For example, first names of people do not count, nor do place and brand names not taken from Spanish culture. So if you used the words *Juan, Coca-Cola*, and *New York City*, expecting them to be six of your thirty words, you would actually only get points for 24 words.

The four areas of the task (Purpose, Vocabulary, Structure, and Word Count) are scored independently. Say that you accomplished the purpose of the task, and also used a nice variety of vocabulary. On the other hand, too many errors in structure make it difficult to understand, and you used fewer than 30 words. You will get a high score for Purpose and Vocabulary, and a low score for Structure and Word Count. Your score will reflect both your strengths and weaknesses.

The strategy

In writing practice during the year prior to the examination, you should try to improve in all areas, so that by the time you take the test you will give yourself the best opportunity to score well in all areas.

What to do at testing time

1. You will be given the situation/context of the task and some specific suggestions about what to include in your note. Read all of this before you begin.

2. You will not have points taken off if you complete the task without using the suggested information. You can write about anything you think of that satisfies the task, and it may be wise to write things that use vocabulary that you are very familiar with. But it may take more time to think of new ideas than it will take to use the suggestions that are presented. Remember, satisfying the task is your primary goal, and the suggestions give an idea of what the testmaker believes is important in order to accomplish that aim.

3. Start by making a scrap copy and then go over it for errors in spelling, verb forms, noun-adjective agreement and word order. Check for a logical beginning, middle and end.

4. Short sentences that are not too grammatically complex might be a good idea if you have trouble with structure.

5. Try not to compose the note in English and then translate it into Spanish. As you have learned throughout the year, everyday expressions in English are usually different from those in Spanish, and what you have tried to do will be obvious to the person scoring your work.

6. Count your words. Adding adjectives or adverbs can increase the count as well as making what you wrote more interesting.

7. Make a careful final copy on the testing answer sheet that includes all your corrections.

Scoring Your Writing Ability

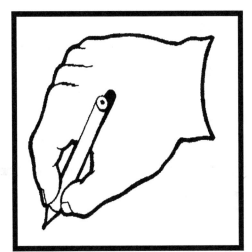

How will your writing be scored? There are four areas in which your writing will be scored: Purpose/Task, Vocabulary, Structure/Conventions, and Word Count. You can get a score of from 0 (lowest) to 4 points (highest) in each of these areas. A score of 0 in any area means the writing did not include enough material for a score of 1 point. Here are the details:

Purpose/Task

4 points:
> You completed what you were asked to do, everything you wrote had to do with the topic, and all the things you wrote made sense together.

3 points:
> You completed what you were asked to do and you included very little that didn't have to do with the topic.

2 points:
> You completed what you were asked to do, but it may not be very clear because you put in some things that have nothing to do with the topic.

1 point:
> You wrote at least one sentence about the topic, but everything else had nothing to do with it.

Vocabulary

4 points:
> You used a lot of different kinds of words to write extra things in your answer. You used many nouns, verbs and adjectives in your answer.

3 points:
> You used different types of words in your answer that were right for the topic.

2 points:
> You used some words that didn't fit the topic.

1 point:
> You used only a few words that were connected to the topic.

Structure

4 points:
> You made almost no mistakes when you conjugated verbs and when you used nouns and adjectives together. You put words in the right order in sentences and didn't make any spelling mistakes. Any mistakes you made didn't make it hard to understand what you wrote.

3 points:
> You made some mistakes, but it still wasn't hard to understand what you wrote.

2 points:
> You made some mistakes, but they were the kind that made it hard to follow what you wrote.

1 point:
> You made so many mistakes that it made it impossible to understand what you wanted to say.

Word Count

4 points:
> You used 30 or more understandable and allowable Spanish words that helped you write about the topic.

3 points:
> You used 25–29 understandable and allowable Spanish words that helped you write about the topic.

2 points:
> You used only 20–24 understandable and allowable Spanish words that helped you write about the topic.

1 point:
> You used only 15–19 understandable and allowable Spanish words that helped you write about the topic.

In each of these areas, you receive a raw score of from 0 to 4 points. Then your teacher will add the raw scores together and convert them into a final task score. Here is the conversion chart:

13 to 16 points = 5

9 to 12 points = 4

6 to 8 points = 3

3 to 5 points = 2

1 to 2 points = 1

0 points = 0

Writing Checklist

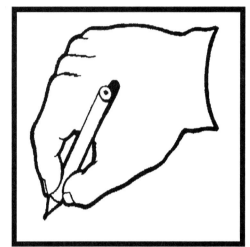

Now that you have read and understood the detailed guidelines, here is the "short form" checklist that your teacher will use to score your writing ability. Learn this well! After you become familiar with it, you might even want to follow this list as you are doing a practice writing activity, and try to give the activity a score.

Purpose/Task

- Did you do what the question asked?
- Did everything you wrote have to do with the topic?
- Did the things you wrote make sense together?

Vocabulary

- Did you use a lot of different kinds of words?
- Did you use words connected to the topic?

4	3	2	1	0

Structure

(Did your mistakes make it hard to understand what you're writing?)

- Did you use the right form of the verbs for different subjects?
- Did you match nouns with the right form of adjectives?
- Did you put the words in the right order in sentences?
- Did you spell all words correctly?

Word Count

- Are all the words understandable?
- Did you use any words in English?
- Is all your writing connected to the topic?
- Did you use 30 or more words?

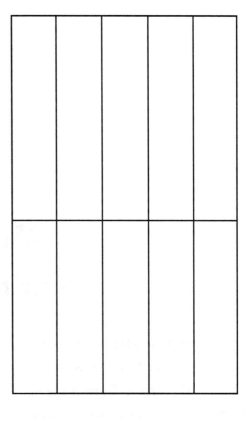

Remember, if your teacher thinks that any part of your writing isn't as good as even the 1-point description, you can get a score of 0 for that portion of your answer. If you don't write at least one sentence that has to do with the topic, your whole answer gets a 0.

In each of these areas, you receive a raw score of from 0 to 4 points. Then your teacher will add the raw scores together and convert them into a final task score. Here is the conversion chart:

13 to 16 points = 5   **9 to 12 points = 4**

6 to 8 points = 3   **3 to 5 points = 2**

1 to 2 points = 1   **0 points = 0**

Part 4
Models for Writing Tasks

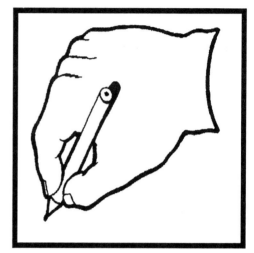

In this section, we will take a look at a sample writing topic and two different student answers. We will show you how each answer would be scored in each of the four different areas.

Topic

You are on vacation and are writing a letter to your cousin telling about your trip. You may wish to include:
- Where you are
- How the weather is
- Activities you are doing
- When you will be home

One of the following answers would receive almost full credit, while the other one is very poorly written. Let's look at the way each one would be scored according to the scoring guidelines your teacher will use.

Example I

Quierdo Juan,

Estoy pasando muy bueno en Puerto Rico. Hace sol y mucho caliente. Todos días voy a una playa bonita con mi hermano y me gusta nadar. Vuelvo a Nueva York la semana que viene.

How was the sample scored?

Purpose/Task   4
This is obviously a letter with salutation. Everything is related to the topic (place, weather, activities, return). The ideas progressed in a logical way from start to finish.

Vocabulary   4
A variety of words was used (present participle, weather expressions, *gustar* with a verb, adjectives, phrase indicating future time). Words related to the topic were used: beach, swim, sunny/warm.

Structure   3
The verbs were conjugated correctly; adjectives agreed with nouns. The words *bueno* and *caliente* were used incorrectly, one article was left out and one word, *querido,* was misspelled. These errors, however, did not make it hard to understand.

Word Count   4
All the words were understandable and fit the topic, although two were incorrectly used. No English words were used. The total allowable words were more than 30.

TOTAL RAW SCORE: 15   5 points for the task

Example II

Yo vacation. Ir swimming y playa baseball. Casa come no mañana. Yo gusto. Mi padres too en New York City por que tiengo escuela.

How was the sample scored?

Purpose/Task   2

You can tell that it is about a trip, although the main clue to that is in English. The parts about parents in New York City and school appear out of place. Since New York City is the only place mentioned, it isn't clear if that's where the vacation is.

Vocabulary   1

Too many English words, although they are meant to fit the topic. No adjectives are used. There are few words related to the topic—even *playa* is used incorrectly to mean play.

Structure   2

All verbs are wrong. One is left out (first sentence); one is not conjugated (*ir*); one is in English (come); and one is misspelled (*tiengo*). Although there were many mistakes, it was just possible to get the overall meaning of what was written, but the mistakes made it hard to follow.

Word Count   1

Since all the English words can't be counted, there are only 15 understandable and allowable words that fit the topic.

TOTAL RAW SCORE: 6   2 points for the task

Part 4
Let's Practice!

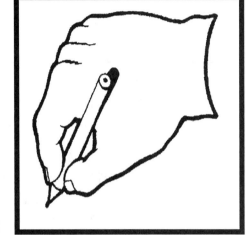

---

1. Topic:

    Your sister's friend is visiting from Venezuela. Write a note inviting her to speak to your Spanish class. You may wish to include statements/questions about:

    - How long your class has been studying Spanish
    - What things you'd like to know about her
    - What her school in Venezuela is like
    - Activities she is doing in the U.S.
    - How she likes the U.S.

---

2. Topic:

    Your school has a Spanish newspaper. Write a letter to the editor. You may wish to include:

    - Whether you find the paper easy to read
    - How you like the paper
    - Your favorite part of the paper
    - An idea for an article/feature
    - How your class uses it

---

3. Topic:

You are a member of a sports team. Write a note to your uncle inviting him to your next game. You might include information on:

- Which sport it is
- Where the game will be played
- The day/time of the game
- How well you play
- Something you can do after the game

4. Topic:

Your friend is in the hospital. You are writing a note to him/her. You might include questions/statements about:

- Regret that s/he is ill
- What's the matter with him/her
- Something that's happening at school
- A wish that s/he feel better

5. Topic:

Write a note to your grandparents about your new pet. You might include information on:

- What kind of pet it is
- A description of the pet
- Name/age of the pet
- How you will take care of it
- How long you have had it

6. Topic:

You stop by your friend's house, but s/he isn't home. You leave this note for your friend. You may wish to include:

- What time you were there
- Why you want to see him/her
- When you'll be home
- That s/he should call you
- That you'll see him/her tomorrow in school

7. Topic:

Your mother is a teacher and you are helping her write a note to a Spanish-speaking parent of a child in her class. You might include information on:

- How the child is doing in class
- Something positive the child does
- Something negative the child does
- How the parent can help the child at home
- When the parent can visit school

8. Topic:

Your school is planning a trip to a Spanish-speaking country for spring vacation and you've signed up to go. Write a letter to a friend telling him/her about the trip. You may wish to include information on:

- When the trip will be
- Where you are going
- How long you'll be away
- What you want to do and see
- How well you will be able to communicate

9. Topic:

Your cousin is coming for a visit and you want him/her to meet your friend. Write a note telling about your friend. You may wish to include:

- A physical description
- What interests they have in common
- Activities they could do
- Your friend's name
- Your friend's age

10. Topic:

A group of students from Spain will be visiting your school. Write a letter telling them about your school. You might include information on:

- The school and facilities
- The number of students
- The subjects taught
- School activities
- What you will show them

11. Topic:

Your family is planning a trip to the Dominican Republic. Write a note to the Tourist Office to get some information. You might include questions/statements about:

- Where you want to visit
- The time of year you plan to go
- Length of stay
- Activities
- Cost of hotels, meals, etc.

12. Topic:

Your class is planning a trip to a Mexican restaurant. Write a note to the restaurant. You might include questions/statements about:

- Date of the trip
- Number of students and teachers
- What food is available
- The cost
- How to reach you with information

13. Topic:

You are going to a friend's house after school to study. Write a note to your mother giving directions so she can pick you up there later. You might include information on:

- Your friend's name and why you are at his/her house
- Address of your friend's house
- Location of the house
- Directions
- Time she should come

14. Topic:

Write a note to a friend to turn down a birthday party invitation because you are ill. You might include statements about:

- Apology
- Why you can't come
- How long you have been sick
- Happy birthday wishes

15. Topic:

Write a short entry for a contest to win a new wardrobe. You might include information on:

- Favorite colors
- Sports clothing you need
- What you usually wear to school
- Summer clothes you need
- Sizes

16. Topic:

Write a note applying to work on the Spanish club's newspaper. You might include information on:

- Why you want the position
- How you are doing in Spanish class
- Available hours
- Why you would be good for the job
- How long you've been studying Spanish

17. Topic:

You are sending a birthday card to a friend who has moved away. Write a short note to add on to the card. You may wish to include questions/statements about:

- Birthday greeting
- How his/her family is
- Some interesting activity you are doing
- What's going on in school
- His/her activities

18. Topic:

Write a note to your parents explaining why you need a larger allowance. You may wish to include information about:

- Your weekly expenses
- What you could do to earn it
- Cost of school lunch
- Something you want to buy for yourself
- Friends' allowances

19. Topic:

Your brother called to say he won't be home after school. Write a note to your parents about his plans. You might include information on:

- Where he is going
- Who he's with
- His plans
- Why he'll be late
- When he'll be home

20. Topic:

Write a note inviting your cousin to go to the movies with you next week. You may wish to include:

- Movie title
- Where it is playing
- Day and time you want to go
- Cost